D0615352

Elements of Semiology

Also by Roland Barthes

ON RACINE
WRITING DEGREE ZERO
MYTHOLOGIES
S/Z
THE PLEASURE OF THE TEXT
SADE / FOURIER / LOYOLA
ROLAND BARTHES

32061730

P
123
B37
1973

Elements of Semiology

Roland Barthes

Translated from the French by
Annette Lavers and Colin Smith

 HILL AND WANG

A division of Farrar, Straus and Giroux

New York

DISCARDED

NORMANDALE COMMUNITY COLLEGE
LIBRARY
9700 FRANCE AVENUE SOUTH
BLOOMINGTON MN 55431-4399

MAY 25 2001

Hill and Wang
A division of Farrar, Straus and Giroux
19 Union Square West, New York 10003

Copyright © 1964 by Editions du Seuil, Paris
Translation copyright © 1967 by Jonathan Cape Ltd.
All rights reserved
Distributed in Canada by Douglas & McIntyre Ltd.
Printed in the United States of America
Library of Congress catalog card number: 68-30769
First published in 1964 by Editions du Seuil, Paris, as *Eléments de Sémiolog*
First American edition published in 1973 by Hill and Wang
Twenty-first printing, 1999

Contents

INTRODUCTION

In his *Course in General Linguistics*, first published in 1916, Saussure postulated the existence of a general science of signs, or Semiology, of which linguistics would form only one part. Semiology therefore aims to take in any system of signs, whatever their substance and limits; images, gestures, musical sounds, objects, and the complex associations of all these, which form the content of ritual, convention or public entertainment: these constitute, if not *languages*, at least systems of signification. There is no doubt that the development of mass communications confers particular relevance today upon the vast field of signifying media, just when the success of disciplines such as linguistics, information theory, formal logic and structural anthropology provide semantic analysis with new instruments. There is at present a kind of demand for semiology, stemming not from the fads of a few scholars, but from the very history of the modern world.

The fact remains that, although Saussure's ideas have made great headway, semiology remains a tentative science. The reason for this may well be simple. Saussure, followed in this by the main semiologists, thought that linguistics merely formed a part of the general science of signs. Now it is far from certain that in the social life of today there are to be found any extensive systems of signs outside human language. Semiology has so far concerned itself with codes of no more than slight interest, such as the Highway Code; the moment we go on to systems where the sociological significance is more than superficial, we are once more confronted with language. It is true that objects, images and patterns of behaviour can signify, and do so on a large scale, but never autonomously; every semiological system has its linguistic admixture. Where there is a visual substance, for example, the meaning is confirmed by being duplicated in a linguistic message (which happens in the case of the cinema, advertising, comic strips, press photography, etc.) so that at least a part of the iconic message is, in terms of structural relationship, either redundant or taken up by the linguistic system. As for collections of objects (clothes, food), they enjoy the status of systems only in so far as they pass through the relay of language, which extracts their signifiers (in the form of nomenclature) and names their signifieds* (in the forms of usages or reasons): we are, much more than in former times, and despite the spread of pictorial illustration, a civilization of the written word. Finally, and in more general terms, it appears increasingly more difficult to conceive a system of images and objects whose *signifieds* can exist independently of language: to perceive what a substance signifies is inevitably to fall back on the individuation of a language: there is no meaning which is not designated, and the world of signifieds is none other than that of language.

Thus, though working at the outset on non-linguistic substances, semiology is required, sooner or later, to find language (in the ordinary sense of the

* We have preferred English to Latin in translating *signifiant* and *signifié*, even at the cost of the inelegant plural 'signifieds'.

term) in its path, not only as a model, but also as component, relay or signified. Even so, such language is not quite that of the linguist: it is a second-order language, with its unities no longer monemes or phonemes, but larger fragments of discourse referring to objects or episodes whose meaning *underlies* language, but can never exist independently of it. Semiology is therefore perhaps destined to be absorbed into a *trans-linguistics*, the materials of which may be myth, narrative, journalism, or on the other hand objects of our civilization, in so far as they are *spoken* (through press, prospectus, interview, conversation and perhaps even the inner language, which is ruled by the laws of imagination). In fact, we must now face the possibility of inverting Saussure's declaration: linguistics is not a part of the general science of signs, even a privileged part, it is semiology which is a part of linguistics: to be precise, it is that part covering the *great signifying unities* of discourse. By this inversion we may expect to bring to light the unity of the research at present being done in anthropology, sociology, psycho-analysis and stylistics round the concept of signification.

Though it will doubtless be required some day to change its character, semiology must first of all, if not exactly take definite shape, at least *try itself out*, explore its possibilities and impossibilities. This is feasible only on the basis of preparatory investigation. And indeed it must be acknowledged in advance that such an investigation is both diffident and rash: diffident because semiological knowledge at present can be only a copy of linguistic knowledge; rash because this knowledge must be applied forthwith, at least as a project, to non-linguistic objects.

The *Elements* here presented have as their sole aim the extraction from linguistics of analytical concepts[1] which we think *a priori* to be sufficiently general to start semiological research on its way. In assembling them, it is not presupposed that they will remain intact during the course of research; nor that semiology will always be forced to follow the linguistic model closely.[2] We are merely suggesting and elucidating a terminology in the hope that it may enable an initial (albeit provisional) order to be introduced into the heterogeneous mass of significant facts. In fact what we purport to do is to furnish a principle of classification of the questions.

These elements of semiology will therefore be grouped under four main headings borrowed from structural linguistics:

    I. *Language and Speech.*
    II. *Signified and Signifier.*
    III. *Syntagm and System.*
    IV. *Denotation and Connotation.*

It will be seen that these headings appear in dichotomic form; the reader will also notice that the binary classification of concepts seems frequent in structural thought,[3] as if the metalanguage of the linguist reproduced, like a mirror, the binary structure of the system it is describing; and we shall point out, as the occasion arises, that it would probably be very instructive to study the pre-eminence of binary classification in the discourse of contemporary social sciences. The taxonomy of these sciences, if it were well known, would undoubtedly provide a great deal of information on what might be called the field of intellectual imagination in our time.

I. LANGUAGE (*LANGUE*) AND SPEECH

I.1. IN LINGUISTICS

I.1.1. *In Saussure:* The (dichotomic) concept of
language/speech is central in Saussure* and was certainly a great novelty in relation to earlier linguistics
which sought to find the causes of historical changes
in the evolution of pronunciation, spontaneous associations and the working of analogy, and was therefore a linguistics of the individual act. In working out
this famous dichotomy, Saussure started from the
'multiform and heterogeneous' nature of language,
which appears at first sight as an unclassifiable reality[4]
the unity of which cannot be brought to light, since
it partakes at the same time of the physical, the physiological, the mental, the individual and the social.
Now this disorder disappears if, from this heterogeneous whole, is extracted a purely social object,
the systematized set of conventions necessary to
communication, indifferent to the *material* of the
signals which compose it, and which is a *language*
(*langue*); as opposed to which *speech* (*parole*) covers
the purely individual part of language (phonation, application of the rules and contingent combinations of
signs).

* The Saussurean notions of *langue* and *parole* present to
the translator into English notorious difficulties, which their

I.1.2. *The language (langue): A language* is therefore,
so to speak, language minus speech: it is at the same
time a social institution and a system of values. As a
social institution, it is by no means an act, and it is
not subject to any premeditation. It is the social
part of language, the individual cannot by himself
either create or modify it; it is essentially a collective
contract which one must accept in its entirety if one
wishes to communicate. Moreover, this social product is autonomous, like a game with its own rules,
for it can be handled only after a period of learning. As a system of values, a language is made of a
certain number of elements, each one of which is at
the same time the equivalent of a given quantity of
things and a term of a larger function, in which are
found, in a differential order, other correlative values:
from the point of view of the language, the sign is
like a coin[5] which has the value of a certain amount
of goods which it allows one to buy, but also has
value in relation to other coins, in a greater or lesser
degree. The institutional and the systematic aspect
are of course connected: it is because a language is a
system of contractual values (in part arbitrary, or,
more exactly, unmotivated) that it resists the modifications coming from a single individual, and is consequently a social institution.

I.1.3. *Speech (parole):* In contrast to the language,
which is both institution and system, *speech* is essen-

extension in the present work does nothing to alleviate. We
have translated *langue* as 'a' or '*the* language', except when
the coupling with 'speech' makes the meaning clear. *Les
paroles*, whether applied to several people or to several semi-
otic systems, has been translated by various periphrases
which we hope do not obscure the identity of meaning.

tially an individual act of selection and actualization; it is made in the first place of the 'combination thanks to which the speaking subject can use the code of the language with a view to expressing his personal thought' (this extended speech could be called *discourse*), and secondly by the 'psycho-physical mechanisms which allow him to exteriorize these combinations.' It is certain that phonation, for instance, cannot be confused with the language; neither the institution nor the system are altered if the individual who resorts to them speaks loudly or softly, with slow or rapid delivery, etc. The combinative aspect of speech is of course of capital importance, for it implies that speech is constituted by the recurrence of identical signs: it is because signs are repeated in successive discourses and within one and the same discourse (although they are combined in accordance with the infinite diversity of various people's speech) that each sign becomes an element of the language; and it is because speech is essentially a combinative activity that it corresponds to an individual act and not to a pure creation.

I.1.4. *The dialectics of language and speech:* Language and speech: each of these two terms of course achieves its full definition only in the dialectical process which unites one to the other: there is no language without speech, and no speech outside language: it is in this exchange that the real linguistic *praxis* is situated, as Merleau-Ponty has pointed out. And V. Brøndal writes, 'A language is a purely abstract entity, a norm which stands above individuals, a set of essential types, which speech actualizes in an infinite variety of ways.'[6] Language and speech are therefore in a relation of reciprocal comprehensiveness. On the one hand, the language is 'the treasure deposited by the practice of speech, in the subjects belonging to the same community' and, since it is a collective summa of individual imprints, it must remain incomplete at the level of each isolated individual: a language does not exist perfectly except in the 'speaking mass'; one cannot handle speech except by drawing on the language. But conversely, a language is possible only starting from speech: historically, speech phenomena always precede language phenomena (it is speech which makes language evolve), and genetically, a language is constituted in the individual through his learning from the environmental speech (one does not teach grammar and vocabulary which are, broadly speaking, the language, to babies). To sum, a language is at the same time the product and the instrument of speech: their relationship is therefore a genuinely dialectical one. It will be noticed (an important fact when we come to semiological prospects) that there could not possibly be (at least according to Saussure) a linguistics of speech, since any speech, as soon as it is grasped as a process of communication, is *already* part of the language: the latter only can be the object of a science. This disposes of two questions at the outset: it is useless to wonder whether speech must be studied *before* the language: the opposite is impossible: one can only study speech straight away inasmuch as it reflects the language (inasmuch as it is 'glottic'). It is just as useless to wonder *at the outset* how to separate the language from speech: this is no preliminary operation, but on the contrary the very essence of linguistic and later semiological investigation: to separate the language from speech means *ipso facto* constituting the problematics of the meaning.

I.1.5. *In Hjelmslev:* Hjelmslev[7] has not thrown over Saussure's conception of *language/speech*, but he has redistributed its terms in a more formal way. Within the language itself (which is still opposed to the act of speech) Hjelmslev distinguishes three planes: i) the *schema*, which is the language as pure form (before choosing this term Hjelmslev hesitated between 'system', 'pattern' or 'framework' for this plane):* this is Saussure's *langue* in the strictest sense of the word. It might mean, for instance, the French *r* as defined phonologically by its place in a series of oppositions; ii) the *norm*, which is the language as material form, after it has been defined by some degree of social realization, but still independent of this realization; it would mean the *r* in oral French, whichever way it is pronounced (but not that of written French); iii) the *usage*, which is the language as a set of habits prevailing in a given society: this would mean the *r* as it is pronounced in some regions. The relations of determination between speech, usage, norm and schema are varied: the norm determines usage and speech; usage determines speech

---

* Hjelmslev himself has suggested English, German and Danish translations for the terms he used in this article, which was written in French and published in the *Cahiers Ferdinand de Saussure*, 2, pp. 24–44 (1943). See *Essais Linguistiques*, p. 81, note 1. *Charpente* was a French alternative for *schéma*, 'pattern' was the English term suggested. But, following Hjelmslev's example when he rejected *système* in order not to give a too specific rendering (ibid., p. 72, note 1), we have preferred here to keep *schema* instead of the very general term 'pattern'. – Translators' note.

but is also determined by it; the schema is determined at the same time by speech, usage and norm. Thus appear (in fact) two fundamental planes: i) the *schema*, the theory of which merges with that of the form[8] and of the linguistic institution; ii) the group *norm-usage-speech*, the theory of which merges with that of the substance[9] and of the execution. As – according to Hjelmslev – norm is a pure methodical abstraction and speech a single concretion ('a transient document'), we find in the end a new dichotomy *schema/usage*, which replaces the couple *language/speech*. This redistribution by Hjelmslev is not without interest, however: it is a radical formalization of the concept of the language (under the name of *schema*) and eliminates concrete speech in favour of a more social concept: *usage*. This formalization of the language and socialization of speech enables us to put all the 'positive' and 'substantial' elements under the heading of speech, and all the differentiating ones under that of the language, and the advantage of this, as we shall see presently, is to remove one of the contradictions brought about by Saussure's distinction between the language and the speech.

I.1.6. *Some problems:* Whatever its usefulness and its fecundity, this distinction nevertheless brings some problems in its wake. Let us mention only three.

Here is the first: is it possible to identify the language with the code and the speech with the message? This identification is impossible according to Hjelmslev's theory. P. Guiraud refuses it for, he says, the conventions of the code are explicit, and those of the language implicit;[10] but it is certainly acceptable in the Saussurean framework, and A. Martinet takes it up.[11]

We encounter an analogous problem if we reflect on the relations between speech and syntagm.[12] Speech, as we have seen, can be defined (outside the variations of intensity in the phonation) as a (varied) combination of (recurrent) signs; but at the level of the language itself, however, there already exist some fixed syntagms (Saussure cites a compound word like *magnanimus*). The threshold which separates the language from speech may therefore be precarious, since it is here constituted by 'a certain degree of combination'. This leads to the question of an analysis of those fixed syntagms whose nature is nevertheless linguistic (glottic) since they are treated as one by paradigmatic variation (Hjelmslev calls this analysis morpho-syntax). Saussure had noticed this phenomenon of transition: 'there is probably also a whole series of sentences which belong to the language, and which the individual no longer has to combine himself.'[13] If these stereotypes belong to the language and no longer to speech, and if it proves true that numerous semiological systems use them to a great extent, then it is a real *linguistics of the syntagm* that we must expect, which will be used for all strongly stereotyped 'modes of writing'.

Finally, the third problem we shall indicate concerns the relations of the language with relevance (that is to say, with the signifying element proper in the unit). The language and relevance have sometimes been identified (by Trubetzkoy himself), thus thrusting outside the language all the non-relevant elements, that is, the combinative variants. Yet this identification raises a problem, for there are combinative variants (which therefore at first sight are a speech phenomenon) which are nevertheless *imposed*, that is to say, arbitrary : in French, it is required by the language that the *l* should be voiceless after a voiceless consonant (*oncle*) and voiced after a voiced consonant (*ongle*) without these facts leaving the realm of phonetics to belong to that of phonology. We see the theoretical consequences : must we admit that, contrary to Saussure's affirmation ('in the language there are only differences'), elements which are not differentiating can all the same belong to the language (to the institution)? Martinet thinks so; Frei attempts to extricate Saussure from the contradiction by localizing the differences in *subphonemes*, so that, for instance, *p* could not be differentiating in itself, but only, in it, the consonantic, occlusive voiceless labial features, etc. We shall not here take sides on this question; from a semiological point of view, we shall only remember the necessity of accepting the existence of syntagms and variations which are not signifying and are yet 'glottic', that is, belonging to the language. This linguistics, hardly foreseen by Saussure, can assume a great importance wherever fixed syntagms (or stereotypes) are found in abundance, which is probably the case in mass-languages, and every time non-signifying variations form a second-order corpus of signifiers, which is the case in strongly connated languages :[14] the rolled *r* is a mere combinative variant at the denotative level, but in the speech of the theatre, for instance, it signals a country accent and therefore is a part of a code, without which the message of 'ruralness' could not be either emitted or perceived.

I.1.7. *The idiolect:* To finish on the subject of *language/speech* in linguistics, we shall indicate two appended concepts isolated since Saussure's day. The first is that of the *idiolect*.[15] This is 'the language inasmuch as it is spoken by a single individual' (Martinet), or again 'the whole set of habits of a single individual at a given moment' (Ebeling). Jakobson has questioned the interest of this notion: the language is always socialized, even at the individual level, for in speaking to somebody one always tries to speak more or less the other's language, especially as far as the vocabulary is concerned ('private property in the sphere of language does not exist'): so the idiolect would appear to be largely an illusion. We shall nevertheless retain from this notion the idea that it can be useful to designate the following realities: i) the language of the aphasic who does not understand other people and does not receive a message conforming to his own verbal patterns; this language, then, would be a pure idiolect (Jakobson); ii) the 'style' of a writer, although this is always pervaded by certain verbal patterns coming from tradition that is, from the community; iii) finally, we can openly broaden the notion, and define the idiolect as the language of a linguistic community, that is, of a group of persons who all interpret in the same way all linguistic statements: the idiolect would then correspond roughly to what we have attempted to describe elsewhere under the name of 'writing'.[16] We can say in general that the hesitations in defining the concept of idiolect only reflect the need for an intermediate entity between speech and language (as was already proved by the *usage* theory in Hjelmslev), or, if you like, the need for a speech which is already institutionalized but not yet radically open to formalization, as the language is.

I.1.8. *Duplex Structures:* If we agree to identify *language/speech* and *code/message*, we must here mention a second appended concept which Jakobson has elaborated under the name of *duplex structures*; we shall do so only briefly, for his exposition of it has been reprinted.[17] We shall merely point out that under the name '*duplex structures*' Jakobson studies certain special cases of the general relation *code/message*: two cases of circularity and two cases of overlapping. i) reported speech, or messages within a message (M/M): this is the general case of indirect styles. ii) proper names: the name signifies any person to whom this name is attributed and the circularity of the code is evident (C/C): *John means a person named John*; iii) cases of autonymy ('*Rat* is a syllable'): the word is here used as its own designation, the message overlaps the code (M/C) – this structure is important, for it covers the 'elucidating interpretations', namely, circumlocutions, synonyms and translations from one language into another; iv) the *shifters* are probably the most interesting double structure: the most ready example is that of the personal pronoun (*I, thou*) an indicial symbol which unites within itself the conventional and the existential bonds: for it is only by virtue of a conventional rule that *I* represents its object (so that *I* becomes *ego* in Latin, *ich* in German, etc.), but on the other hand, since it designates the person who utters it, it can only refer existentially to the utterance (C/M). Jakobson reminds us that personal pronouns have long been thought to be the most primitive layer of language

(Humboldt), but that in his view, they point rather to a complex and adult relationship between the code and the message: the personal pronouns are the last elements to be acquired in the child's speech and the first to be lost in aphasia; they are terms of transference which are difficult to handle. The *shifter* theory seems as yet to have been little exploited; yet it is, *a priori*, very fruitful to observe the code struggling with the message, so to speak (the converse being much more commonplace); perhaps (this is only a working hypothesis) it is on this side, that of the *shifters*, which are, as we saw, indicial symbols according to Peirce's terminology, that we should seek the semiological definition of the messages which stand on the frontiers of language, notably certain forms of literary discourse.

I.2. SEMIOLOGICAL PROSPECTS

I.2.1. *The language, speech and the social sciences.* The sociological scope of the *language/speech* concept is obvious. The manifest affinity of the language according to Saussure and of Durkheim's conception of a collective consciousness independent of its individual manifestations has been emphasized very early on. A direct influence of Durkheim on Saussure has even been postulated; it has been alleged that Saussure had followed very closely the debate between Durkheim and Tarde and that his conception of the language came from Durkheim while that of speech was a kind of concession to Tarde's idea on the individual element.[18] This hypothesis has lost some of its topicality because linguistics has chiefly developed, in the Saussurean idea of the language, the 'system of values' aspect, which led to acceptance of the necessity for an immanent analysis of the linguistic institution, and this immanence is inimical to sociological research.

Paradoxically, it is not therefore in the realm of sociology that the best development of the notion of *language/speech* will be found; it is in philosophy, with Merleau-Ponty, who was probably one of the first French philosophers to become interested in Saussure. He took up again the Saussurean distinction as an opposition between *speaking speech* (a signifying intention in its nascent state) and *spoken speech* (an 'acquired wealth' of the language which does recall Saussure's 'treasure').[19] He also broadened the notion by postulating that any *process* presupposes a *system*:[20] thus there has been elaborated an opposition between *event* and *structure* which has become accepted[21] and whose fruitfulness in history is well known.[22]

Saussure's notion has, of course, also been taken over and elaborated in the field of anthropology. The reference to Saussure is too explicit in the whole work of Claude Lévi-Strauss for us to need to insist on it; we shall simply remind the reader of three facts: i) That the opposition between process and system (speech and language) is found again in a concrete guise in the transition from the exchange of women to the structures of kinship; ii) that for Lévi-Strauss this opposition has an epistemological value: the study of linguistic phenomena is the domain of mechanistic (in Lévi-Strauss's sense of the word, namely, as opposed to 'statistical') and structural interpretation, and the study of speech phenomena is the domain of the theory of probabilities (macro-linguistics);[23] iii) finally, that the *unconscious* character of the language in those who draw on it for their speech, which is explicitly postulated by Saussure,[24] is again found in one of the most original and fruitful contentions of Lévi-Strauss, which states that it is not the contents which are unconscious (this is a criticism of Jung's archetypes) but the forms, that is, the symbolical function.

This idea is akin to that of Lacan, according to whom the libido itself is articulated as a system of significations, from which there follows, or will have to follow, a new type of description of the collective field of imagination, not by means of its 'themes', as has been done until now, but by its forms and its functions. Or let us say, more broadly but more clearly : by its signifiers more than by its signifieds.

It can be seen from these brief indications how rich in extra- or meta-linguistic developments the notion *language/speech* is. We shall therefore postulate that there exists a general category *language/speech*, which embraces all the systems of signs; since there are no better ones, we shall keep the terms *language* and *speech*, even when they are applied to communications whose substance is not verbal.

I.2.2. *The garment system:* We saw that the separation between the language and speech represented the essential feature of linguistic analysis; it would therefore be futile to propose to apply this separation straightaway to systems of objects, images or behaviour patterns which have not yet been studied from a semantic point of view. We can merely, in the case of some of these hypothetical systems, fore-see that certain classes of facts will belong to the category of the *language* and others to that of *speech*, and make it immediately clear that in the course of its application to semiology, Saussure's distinction is likely to undergo modifications which it will be pre-cisely our task to note.

Let us take the garment system for instance; it is probably necessary to subdivide it into three different systems, according to which substance is used for communication.

In clothes as *written* about, that is to say described in a fashion magazine by means of articulated lan-guage, there is practically no 'speech': the garment which is described never corresponds to an individual handling of the rules of fashion, it is a systematized set of signs and rules: it is a language in its pure state. According to the Saussurean schema, a language without speech would be impossible; what makes the fact acceptable here is, on the one hand, that the language of fashion does not emanate from the 'speaking mass' but from a group which makes the decisions and deliberately elaborates the code, and on the other hand that the abstraction inherent in any language is here materialized as written language: fashion clothes (as written about) are the language at the level of vestimentary communication and speech at the level of verbal communication.

In clothes as *photographed* (if we suppose, to simplify matters, that there is no duplication by verbal description), the language still issues from the fashion group, but it is no longer given in a wholly abstract form, for a photographed garment is always worn by an individual woman. What is given by the fashion photograph is a semi-formalized state of the garment system: for on the one hand, the language of fashion must here be inferred from a pseudo-real garment, and on the other, the wearer of the garment (the photographed model) is, so to speak, a normative individual, chosen for her canonic generality, and who consequently represents a 'speech' which is fixed and devoid of all combinative freedom.

Finally in clothes as *worn* (or real clothes), as Trubetzkoy had suggested,[25] we again find the classic distinction between language and speech. The language, in the garment system, is made i) by the oppositions of pieces, parts of garment and 'details', the variation of which entails a change in meaning (to wear a beret or a bowler hat does not have the same meaning); ii) by the rules which govern the association of the pieces among themselves, either on the length of the body or in depth. Speech, in the garment system, comprises all the phenomena of anomic fabrication (few are still left in our society) or of individual way of wearing (size of the garment, degree of cleanliness or wear, personal quirks, free association of pieces). As for the dialectic which unites here costume (the language) and clothing (speech), it does not resemble that of verbal language; true, clothing always draws on costume (except in the case of eccentricity, which, by the way, also has its signs), but costume, at least today, *precedes* clothing, since it comes from the ready-made industry, that is, from a minority group (although more anonymous than that of Haute Couture).

I.2.3. *The food system:* Let us now take another signifying system: food. We shall find there without difficulty Saussure's distinction. The alimentary language is made of i) rules of exclusion (alimentary taboos); ii) signifying oppositions of units, the type of which remains to be determined (for instance the type *savoury/sweet*); iii) rules of association, either simultaneous (at the level of a dish) or successive (at the level of a menu); iv) rituals of use which function, perhaps, as a kind of alimentary *rhetoric*. As for alimentary 'speech', which is very rich, it comprises all the personal (or family) variations of preparation and association (one might consider cookery within one family, which is subject to a number of habits, as an idiolect). The *menu*, for instance, illustrates very well this relationship between the language and speech : any menu is concocted with reference to a structure (which is both national – or regional – and social); but this structure is filled differently according to the days and the users, just as a linguistic 'form' is filled by the free variations and combinations which a speaker needs for a particular message. The relationship between the language and speech would here be fairly similar to that which is found in verbal language : broadly, it is usage, that is to say, a sort of sedimentation of many people's speech, which makes up the alimentary language; however, phenomena of individual innovation can acquire an institutional value within it. What is missing, in any case, contrary to what happened in the garment system, is the action of a deciding group : the alimentary language is evolved only from a broadly collective usage, or from a purely individual speech.

I.2.4. *The car system, the furniture system:* To bring to a close, somewhat arbitrarily, this question of the prospects opened up by the *language/speech* distinction, we shall mention a few more suggestions concerning two systems of objects, very different, it is true, but which have in common a dependence in each case on a deciding and manufacturing group: cars and furniture.

In the car system, the language is made up by a whole set of forms and details, the structure of which is established differentially by comparing the prototypes to each other (independently of the number of their 'copies'); the scope of 'speech' is very narrow because, for a given status of buyer, freedom in choosing a model is very restricted: it can involve only two or three models, and within each model, colour and fittings. But perhaps we should here exchange the notion of cars as *objects* for that of cars as sociological facts; we would then find in the *driving* of cars the variations in usage of the object which usually make up the plane of speech. For the user cannot in this instance have a direct action on the model and combine its units; his freedom of interpretation is found in the usage developed in time and within which the 'forms' issuing from the language must, in order to become actual, be relayed by certain practices.

Finally, the last system about which we should like to say a word, that of furniture, is also a semantic object: the 'language' is formed both by the oppositions of functionally identical pieces (two types of wardrobe, two types of bed, etc), each of which, according to its 'style', refers to a different meaning, and by the rules of association of the different units at the level of a room ('furnishing'); the 'speech' is here formed either by the insignificant variations which the user can introduce into one unit (by tinkering with one element, for instance), or by freedom in associating pieces of furniture together.

I.2.5. *Complex systems:* The most interesting systems, at least among those which belong to the province of mass-communications, are complex systems in which different substances are engaged. In cinema, television and advertising, the senses are subjected to the concerted action of a collection of images, sounds and written words. It will, therefore, be premature to decide, in their case, which facts belong to the language and which belong to speech, on the one hand as long as one has not discovered whether the 'language' of each of these complex systems is original or only compounded of the subsidiary 'languages' which have their places in them, and on the other hand as long as these subsidiary languages have not been analysed (we know the linguistic 'language', but not that of images or that of music).

As for the Press, which can be reasonably considered as an autonomous signifying system, even if we confine ourselves to its written elements only, we are still almost entirely ignorant of a linguistic phenomenon which seems to play an essential part in it: connotation, that is, the development of a system of second-order meanings, which are so to speak parasitic on the language proper.[26] This second-order system is also a 'language', within which there develop speech-phenomena, idiolects and duplex structures. In the case of such complex or connoted systems (both characteristics are not mutually exclusive), it is therefore no longer possible to predetermine, even in global and hypothetical fashion, what belongs to the language and what belongs to speech.

I.2.6. *Problems (1) – the origin of the various signifyings systems:* The semiological extension of the *language/speech* notion brings with it some problems, which of course coincide with the points where the linguistic model can no longer be followed and must be altered. The first problem concerns the origin of the various systems, and thus touches on the very dialectics of language and speech. In the linguistic model, nothing enters the language without having been tried in speech, but conversely no speech is possible (that is, fulfils its function of communication) if it is not drawn from the 'treasure' of the language. This process is still, at least partially, found in a system like that of food, although individual innovations brought into it can become language phenomena. But in most other semiological systems, the language is elaborated not by the 'speaking mass' but by a deciding group. In this sense, it can be held that in most semiological languages, the sign is really and truly 'arbitrary'[27] since it is founded in artificial fashion by a unilateral decision; these in fact are fabricated languages, 'logo-techniques'. The user follows these languages, draws messages (or 'speech') from them but has no part in their elaboration. The deciding group which is at the origin of the system (and of its changes) can be more or less narrow; it can be a highly qualified technocracy (fashion, motor industry); it can also be a more diffuse and anonymous group (the production of standardized furniture, the middle reaches of ready-to-wear). If, however, this artificial character does not alter the insti-

tutional nature of the communication and preserves
some amount of dialectical play between the system
and usage, it is because, in the first place, although
imposed on the users, the signifying 'contract' is no
less observed by the great majority of them (otherwise
the user is *marked* with a certain 'asociability': he
can no longer communicate anything except his
eccentricity); and because, moreover, languages
elaborated as the outcome of a decision are not entirely free ('arbitrary'). They are subject to the determination of the community, at least through the
following agencies: i) when new needs are born, following the development of societies (the move to semi-
European clothing in contemporary African countries,
the birth of new patterns of quick feeding in in-
dustrial and urban societies); ii) when economic
requirements bring about the disappearance or pro-
motion of certain materials (artificial textiles); iii)
when ideology limits the invention of forms, subjects it to taboos and reduces, so to speak, the margins of the 'normal'. In a wider sense, we can say
that the elaborations of deciding groups, namely the
logo-techniques, are themselves only the terms of an
ever-widening function, which is the collective field
of imagination of the epoch: thus individual innovation is transcended by a sociological determination (from restricted groups), but these sociological
determinations refer in turn to a final meaning, which
is anthropological.

I.2.7. *Problems (II) – the proportion between 'language' and 'speech' in the various systems:* The
second problem presented by the semiological extension of the *language/speech* notion is centred on the

proportion, in the matter of volume, which can be established between the 'language' and the corresponding 'speech' in any system. In verbal language there is a very great disproportion between the language, which is a finite set of rules, and speech, which comes under the heading of these rules and is practically unlimited in its variety. It can be presumed that the food system still offers an important difference in the volume of each, since within the culinary 'forms', the modalities and combinations in interpretation are numerous. But we have seen that in the car or the furniture system the scope for combinative variations and free associations is small: there is very little margin – at least of the sort which is acknowledged by the institution itself – between the model and its 'execution': these are systems in which 'speech' is poor. In a particular system, that of written fashion, speech is even almost non-existent, so that we are dealing here, paradoxically, with a language without speech (which is possible, as we have seen, only because this language is upheld by linguistic speech).

The fact remains that if it is true that there are languages without speech or with a very restricted speech, we shall have to revise the Saussurean theory which states that a language is nothing but a system of differences (in which case, being entirely negative, it cannot be grasped outside speech). and complete the couple *language/speech* with a third, presignifying element, a matter or substance providing the (necessary) support of signification. In a phrase like *a long or short dress*, the 'dress' is only the support of a variant (*long/short*) which *does* fully belong to the garment language – a distinction which is unknown in ordinary language, in which, since the sound is considered as *immediately* significant, it cannot be decomposed into an inert and a semantic element. This would lead us to recognize in (non-linguistic) semiological systems three (and not two) planes: that of the matter, that of the language and that of the usage. This of course allows us to account for systems without 'execution', since the first element ensures that there is a materiality of the language; and such a modification is all the more plausible since it can be explained genetically: if, in such systems, the 'language' needs a 'matter' (and no longer a 'speech'), it is because unlike that of human language their origin is in general utilitarian, and not signifying.

II. SIGNIFIER AND SIGNIFIED

II.1. THE SIGN

II.1.1. *The classification of signs:* The signified and the signifier, in Saussurean terminology, are the components of the *sign*. Now this term, *sign*, which is found in very different vocabularies (from that of theology to that of medicine), and whose history is very rich (running from the Gospels[28] to cybernetics), is for these very reasons very ambiguous; so before we come back to the Saussurean acceptance of the word, we must say a word about the notional field in which it occupies a place, albeit imprecise, as will be seen. For, according to the arbitrary choice of various authors, the sign is placed in a series of terms which have affinities and dissimilarities with it: *signal, index, icon, symbol, allegory,* are the chief rivals of *sign.* Let us first state the element which is common to all these terms: they all necessarily refer us to a *relation* between two *relata*.[29] This feature cannot therefore be used to distinguish any of the terms in the series; to find a variation in meaning, we shall have to resort to other features, which will be expressed here in the form of an alternative (*presence/absence*): i) the relation implies, or does not imply, the mental representation of one of the *relata*; ii) the relation implies, or does not imply, an analogy between the *relata*; iii) the link between the two *relata* (the stimulus and its response) is immediate or is not; iv) the *relata* exactly coincide or, on the contrary, one overruns the other; v) the relation implies, or does not imply, an existential connection with the user.[30] Whether these features are positive or negative (marked or unmarked), each term in the field is differentiated from its neighbours. It must be added that the distribution of the field varies from one author to another, a fact which produces terminological contradictions; these will be easily seen at a glance from a table of the incidence of features and terms in four different authors: Hegel, Peirce, Jung and Wallon (the reference to some features, whether marked or unmarked, may be absent in some authors). We see that the terminological contradiction bears essentially on *index* (for Peirce, the index is existential, for Wallon, it is not) and on *symbol* (for Hegel and Wallon there is a relation of analogy – or of 'motivation' – between the two *relata* of the symbol, but not for Peirce; moreover, for Peirce, the symbol is not existential, whereas it is for Jung). But we see also that these contradictions – which in this table are read vertically – are very well explained, or rather, that they compensate each other through transfers of meaning from term to term in the same author. These transfers can here be read horizontally: for instance, the symbol is analogical in Hegel as opposed to the sign which is not; and if it is not in Peirce, it is because the icon can absorb that feature. All this means, to sum up and talk in semiological terms (this being the point of this brief analysis which reflects, like a mirror, the subject and methods of our study), that the words in the field derive their

36

	signal	index	icon	symbol	sign	allegory
1. Mental representation	Wallon −	Wallon −		Wallon +	Wallon +	
2. Analogy			Peirce +	Hegel + Wallon + Peirce −	Hegel − Wallon −	
3. Immediacy	Wallon +	Wallon −				
4. Adequacy				Hegel − Jung − Wallon −	Hegel + Jung + Wallon +	
5. Existential aspect	Wallon +	Wallon − Peirce +		Peirce − Jung +		Jung −

meaning only from their opposition to one another (usually in pairs), and that if these oppositions are preserved, the meaning is unambiguous. In particular, *signal* and *index*, *symbol* and *sign*, are the terms of two different functions, which can themselves be opposed as a whole, as they do in Wallon, whose terminology is the clearest and the most complete[31] (*icon* and *allegory* are confined to the vocabulary of Peirce and Jung). We shall therefore say, with Wallon, that the *signal* and the *index* form a group of *relata* devoid of mental representation, whereas in the opposite group, that of *symbol* and *sign*, this representation exists; furthermore, the *signal* is immediate and existential, whereas the *index* is not (it is only a trace); finally, that in the *symbol* the representation is analogical and inadequate (Christianity 'outruns' the cross), whereas in the *sign* the relation is unmotivated and exact (there is no analogy between the word *ox* and the image of an *ox*, which is perfectly covered by its *relatum*).

II.1.2. *The linguistic sign:* In linguistics, the notion of sign does not give rise to any competition between neighbouring terms. When he sought to designate the signifying relationship, Saussure immediately eliminated *symbol* (because the term implied the idea of motivation) in favour of *sign* which he defined as the union of a signifier and a signified (in the fashion of the recto and verso of a sheet of paper), or else of an acoustic image and a concept. Until he found the words *signifier* and *signified*, however, *sign* remained ambiguous, for it tended to become identified with the signifier only, which Saussure wanted at all costs to avoid; after having hesitated between *sôme* and

sème, form and *idea, image* and *concept,* Saussure
settled upon *signifier* and *signified,* the union of which
forms the sign. This is a paramount proposition,
which one must always bear in mind, for there is a
tendency to interpret *sign* as signifier, whereas this
is a two-sided Janus-like entity. The (important) con-
sequence is that, for Saussure, Hjelmslev and Frei at
least, since the signifieds are signs among others,
semantics must be a part of structural linguistics,
whereas for the American mechanists the signifieds
are substances which must be expelled from linguistics and left to psychology. Since Saussure, the theory
of the linguistic sign has been enriched by the *double
articulation* principle, the importance of which has
been shown by Martinet, to the extent that he made
it the criterion which defines language. For among
linguistic signs, we must distinguish between the
significant units, each one of which is endowed with
one meaning (the 'words', or to be exact, the
'monemes') and which form the first articulation, and
the *distinctive units,* which are part of the form but
do not have a direct meaning ('the sounds', or rather
the phonemes), and which constitute the second
articulation. It is this double articulation which
accounts for the economy of human language; for
it is a powerful gearing-down which allows, for instance, American Spanish to produce, with only 21
distinctive units, 100,000 significant units.

II.1.3. *Form and substance:* The sign is therefore a
compound of a signifier and a signified. The plane of
the signifiers constitutes the *plane of expression* and
that of the signifieds the *plane of content.* Within
each of these two planes, Hjelmslev has introduced a

39

distinction which may be important for the study of the semiological (and no longer only linguistic) sign. According to him, each plane comprises two *strata*: *form* and *substance*; we must insist on the new definition of these two terms, for each of them has a weighty lexical past. The *form* is what can be described exhaustively, simply and coherently (epistemological criteria) by linguistics without resorting to any extralinguistic premise; the *substance* is the whole set of aspects of linguistic phenomena which cannot be described without resorting to extralinguistic premises. Since both *strata* exist on the plane of expression and the plane of content, we therefore have: i) a substance of expression: for instance the phonic, articulatory, non-functional substance which is the field of phonetics, not phonology; ii) a form of expression, made of the paradigmatic and syntactic rules (let us note that the same form can have two different substances, one phonic, the other graphic); iii) a substance of content: this includes, for instance, the emotional, ideological, or simply notional aspects of the signified, its 'positive' meaning; iv) a form of content: it is the formal organization of the signified among themselves through the absence or presence of a semantic mark.[32] This last notion is difficult to grasp, because of the impossibility of separating the signifiers from the signifieds in human language; but for this very reason the subdivision *form/substance* can be made more useful and easier to handle in semiology, in the following cases: i) when we deal with a system in which the signifieds are substantified in a substance other than that of their own system (this is, as we have seen, the case with fashion as it is written about); ii) when a system of objects includes a substance which is not immediately and functionally significant, but can be, at a certain level, simply utilitarian: the function of a dish can be to signify a situation and also to serve as food.

II.1.4. *The semiological sign:* This perhaps allows us to foresee the nature of the semiological sign in relation to the linguistic sign. The semiological sign is also, like its model, compounded of a signifier and a signified (the colour of a light, for instance, is an order to move on, in the Highway Code), but it differs from it at the level of its substances. Many semiological systems (objects, gestures, pictorial images)[33] have a substance of expression whose essence is not to signify; often, they are objects of everyday use, used by society in a derivative way, to signify something: clothes are used for protection and food for nourishment even if they are also used as signs. We propose to call these semiological signs, whose origin is utilitarian and functional, *sign-functions.* The sign-function bears witness to a double movement, which must be taken apart. In a first stage (this analysis is purely operative and does not imply real temporality) the function becomes pervaded with meaning. This semantization is inevitable: *as soon as there is a society, every usage is converted into a sign of itself;* the use of a raincoat is to give protection from the rain, but this use cannot be dissociated from the very signs of an atmospheric situation. Since our society produces only standardized, normalized objects, these objects are unavoidably realizations of a model, the speech of a language, the substances of a significant form. To rediscover a non-signifying object, one

would have to imagine a utensil absolutely impro-
vised and with no similarity to an existing model
(Lévi-Strauss has shown to what extent tinkering
about is itself the search for a meaning): a hypothesis
which is virtually impossible to verify in any society.
This universal semantization of the usages is crucial:
it expresses the fact that there is no reality except
when it is intelligible, and should eventually lead to
the merging of sociology with socio-logic.[34] But once
the sign is constituted, society can very well re-
functionalize it, and speak about it as if it were an
object made for use: a fur-coat will be described as
if it served only to protect from the cold. This recurrent functionalization, which needs, in order to
exist, a second-order language, is by no means the
same as the first (and indeed purely ideal) functionalization: for the function which is re-presented does
in fact correspond to a second (disguised) semantic
institutionalization, which is of the order of connotation. The sign-function therefore has (probably) an
anthropological value, since it is the very unit where
the relations of the technical and the significant are
woven together.

II.2. THE SIGNIFIED

II.2.1. *Nature of the signified:* In linguistics, the
nature of the signified has given rise to discussions
which have centred chiefly on its degree of 'reality';
all agree, however, on emphasizing the fact that the
signified is not 'a thing' but a mental representation
of the 'thing'. We have seen that in the definition of
the sign by Wallon, this representative character was

a relevant feature of the sign and the symbol (as opposed to the index and the signal). Saussure himself has clearly marked the mental nature of the signified by calling it a *concept*: the signified of the word *ox* is not the animal *ox*, but its mental image (this will prove important in the subsequent discussion on the nature of the sign).[35] These discussions, however, still bear the stamp of psychologism, so the analysis of the Stoics[36] will perhaps be thought preferable. They carefully distinguished the φαντασία λογική (the mental representation), the τυγχανόν (the real thing) and the λεκτόν (the utterable). The signified is neither the φαντασία nor the τυγχανόν, but rather the λεκτυν; being neither an act of consciousness, nor a real thing, it can be defined only within the signifying process, in a quasi-tautological way: it is this 'something' which is meant by the person who uses the sign. In this way we are back again to a purely functional definition: the signified is one of the two *relata* of the sign; the only difference which opposes it to the signified is that the latter is a mediator. The situation could not be essentially different in semiology, where objects, images, gestures, etc., inasmuch as they are significant, refer back to something which can be expressed only through them, except that the semiological signified can be taken up by the linguisitic signs. One can say, for instance, that a certain sweater means *long autumn walks in the woods*; in this case, the signified is mediated not only by its vestimentary signifier (the sweater), but also by a fragment of speech (which greatly helps in handling it). We could give the name of *isology* to the phenomenon whereby language wields its signifiers and signifieds so that it

43

is impossible to dissociate and differentiate them, in order to set aside the case of the non-isologic systems (which are inevitably complex), in which the signified can be simply *juxtaposed* with its signifier.

II.2.2. *Classification of the linguistic signifieds:* How can we classify the signifieds? We know that in semiology this operation is fundamental, since it amounts to isolating the *form* from the content. As far as linguistic signifiers are concerned, two sorts of classification can be conceived. The first is external, and makes use of the 'positive' (and not purely differential) content of concepts: this is the case in the methodical groupings of Hallig and Wartburg,[37] and in the more convincing notional fields of Trier and lexicological fields of Matoré.[38] But from a structural point of view, this classification (especially those of Hallig and Wartburg) have the defect of resting still too much on the (ideological) *substance* of the signifieds, and not on their *form*. To succeed in establishing a really formal classification, one would have to succeed in reconstituting oppositions of signifieds, and in isolating, within each one of these, a relevant commutative feature:[39] this method has been advocated by Hjelmslev, Sörensen, Prieto and Greimas. Hjelmslev, for instance, decomposes a moneme like 'mare' into two smaller significant units: 'Horse' + 'female', and these units can be commutated and therefore used to reconstitute new monemes ('pig' + 'female' = 'sow', 'horse' + 'male' = 'stallion'); Prieto sees in 'vir' two commutable features 'homo' + 'masculus'; Sörensen reduces the lexicon of kinship to a combination of 'primitives' ('father' = male parent, 'parent' = first ascendent). None of these

44

analyses has yet been developed.[40] Finally, we must remind the reader that according to some linguists, the signifieds are not a part of linguistics, which is concerned only with signifiers, and that semantic classification lies outside the field of linguistics.[41]

II.2.3. *The semiological signifieds:* Structural linguistics, however advanced, has not yet elaborated a semantics, that is to say a classification of the *forms* of the verbal signified. One may therefore easily imagine that it is at present impossible to put forward a classification of semiological signifieds, unless we choose to fall back on to known notional fields. We shall venture three observations only.

The first concerns the mode of actualization of semiological signifieds. These can occur either isologically or not; in the latter case, they are taken up, through articulated language, either by a word (*week-end*) or by a group of words (*long walks in the country*); they are thereby easier to handle, since the analyst is not forced to impose on them his own metalanguage, but also more dangerous, since they ceaselessly refer back to the semantic classification of the language itself (which is itself unknown), and not to a classification having its bases in the system under observation. The signifieds of the fashion garment, even if they are mediated by the speech of the magazine, are not necessarily distributed like the signifieds of the language, since they do not always have the same 'length' (here a word, there a sentence). In the first case, that of the isologic systems, the signified has no materialization other than its typical signifier; one cannot therefore handle it except by imposing on it a metalanguage. One can for instance ask some subjects about the meaning they attribute to a piece of music by submitting to them a list of verbalized signifieds (*anguished, stormy, sombre, tormented,* etc.);[42] whereas in fact all these verbal signs for a single musical signified, which ought to be designated by one single cipher, which would imply no verbal dissection and no metaphorical small change. These metalanguages, issuing from the analyst in the former case, and the system itself in the latter, are probably inevitable, and this is what still makes the analysis of the signifieds, or ideological analysis, problematical; its place within the semiological project will at least have to be defined in theory.

Our second remark concerns the extension of the semiological signifieds. The whole of the signifieds of a system (once formalized) constitutes a great function; now it is probable that from one system to the other, the great semiological functions not only communicate, but also partly overlap; the form of the signified in the garment system is probably partly the same as that of the signified in the food system, being, as they are, both articulated on the large-scale opposition of work and festivity, activity and leisure. One must therefore foresee a total ideological description, common to all the systems of a given synchrony.

Finally – and this will be our third remark – we may consider that to each system of signifiers (lexicons) there corresponds, on the plane of the signifieds, a corpus of practices and techniques; these collections of signifieds imply on the part of system consumers (of 'readers', that is to say), different degrees of knowledge (according to differences in their 'culture'), which explains how the same 'lexie' (or large unit of reading) can be deciphered differently according to the individuals concerned, without ceasing to belong to a given 'language'. Several lexicons – and consequently several bodies of signifieds – can coexist within the same individual, determining in each one more or less 'deep' readings.

II.3. THE SIGNIFIER

II.3.1. *Nature of the signifier:* The nature of the signifier suggests roughly the same remarks as that of the signified: it is purely a *relatum*, whose definition cannot be separated from that of the signified. The only difference is that the signifier is a mediator: some matter is necessary to it. But on the one hand it is not sufficient to it, and on the other, in semiology, the signifier can, too, be relayed by a certain matter: that of words. This materiality of the signifier makes it once more necessary to distinguish clearly *matter* from *substance*: a substance can be immaterial (in the case of the substance of the content); therefore, all one can say is that the substance of the signifier is always material (sounds, objects, images). In semiology, where we shall have to deal with mixed systems in which different kinds of matter are involved (sound and image, object and writing, etc.), it may be appropriate to collect together all the signs, *inasmuch as they are borne by one and the same matter,* under the concept of the *typical sign*: the verbal sign, the graphic sign, the iconic sign, the gestural sign are all typical signs.

II.3.2. *Classification of the signifiers:* The classification of the signifiers is nothing but the structuralization proper of the system. What has to be done is to cut up the 'endless' message constituted by the whole of the messages emitted at the level of the studied corpus, into minimal significant units by means of the commutation test,[43] then to group these units into paradigmatic classes, and finally to classify the syntagmatic relations which link these units. These operations constitute an important part of the semiological undertaking which will be dealt with in chapter III; we anticipate the point in mentioning it here.[44]

II.4. THE SIGNIFICATION

II.4.1. *The significant correlation:* The sign is a (two-faced) slice of sonority, visuality, etc. The *signification* can be conceived as a process; it is the act which binds the signifier and the signified, an act whose product is the sign. This distinction has, of course, only a classifying (and not phenomenological) value: firstly, because the union of signifier and signified, as we shall see, does not exhaust the semantic act, for the sign derives its value also from its surroundings; secondly, because, probably, the mind does not proceed, in the semantic process, by conjunction but by carving out.[45] And indeed the signification (*semiosis*) does not unite unilateral entities, it does not conjoin two terms, for the very good reason that signifier and signified are both at once term and relation.[46] This ambiguity makes any graphic representation of the signification somewhat clumsy, yet this operation is

48

necessary for any semiological discourse. On this point, let us mention the following attempts:

1) $\frac{Sr}{Sd}$: In Saussure, the sign appears, in his demonstration, as the vertical extension of a situation *in depth* : in the language, the signified is, as it were, *behind* the signifier, and can be reached only through it, although, on the one hand, these excessively spatial metaphors miss the dialectical nature of the signification, and on the other hand the 'closed' character of the sign is acceptable only for the frankly discontinuous systems, such as that of the language.

2) ERC: Hjelmslev has chosen in preference a purely graphic representation: there is a relation (R) between the plane of expression (E) and the plane of content (C). This formula enables us to account economically and without metaphorical falsification, for the metalanguages or derivative systems E R (ERC).[47]

3) $\frac{S}{s}$: Lacan, followed by Laplanche and Leclaire,[48] uses a spatialized writing which, however, differs from Saussure's representation on two points: i) the signifier (S) is global, made up of a multilevelled chain (metaphorical chain): signifier and signified have only a floating relationship and coincide only at certain anchorage points; ii) the line between the signifier (S) and the signified (s) has its own value (which of course it had not in Saussure): it represents the repression of the signified.

4) Sr $\equiv$ Sd : Finally, in non-isologic systems (that is, those in which the signifieds are materialized through another system), it is of course legitimate to extend

the relation in the form of an equivalence ($\equiv$) but not of an identity ($=$).

II.4.2. *The arbitrary and the motivated in linguistics:* We have seen that all that could be said about the signifier is that it was a (material) mediator of the signified. What is the nature of this mediation? In linguistics, this problem has provoked some discussion, chiefly about terminology, for all is fairly clear about the main issues (this will perhaps not be the case with semiology). Starting from the fact that in human language the choice of sounds is not imposed on us by the meaning itself (the *ox* does not determine the sound *ox*, since in any case the sound is different in other languages), Saussure had spoken of an *arbitrary* relation between signifier and signified. Benveniste has questioned the aptness of this word:[49] what is arbitrary is the relation between the signifier and the 'thing' which is signified (of the sound *ox* and the animal the *ox*). But, as we have seen, even for Saussure, the sign is not the 'thing', but the mental representation of the thing (*concept*); the association of sound and representation is the outcome of a collective training (for instance the learning of the French tongue); this association – which is the signification – is by no means arbitrary (for no French person is free to modify it), indeed it is, on the contrary, necessary. It was therefore suggested to say that in linguistics the signification is *unmotivated*. This lack of motivation, is, by the way, only partial (Saussure speaks of a relative analogy): from signified to signifier, there is a certain motivation in the (restricted) case of onomatopoeia, as we shall see shortly, and also every time a series of signs is created by the tongue through the imitation of a certain prototype of composition or derivation: this is the case with so-called proportional signs: *pommier, poirer, abricotier*, etc., once the lack of motivation in their roots and their suffix is established, show an analogy in their composition. We shall therefore say in general terms that in the language the link between signifier and signified is contractual in its principle, but that this contract is collective, inscribed in a long temporality (Saussure says that 'a language is always a legacy'), and that consequently it is, as it were, *naturalized*; in the same way, Levi-Strauss specified that the linguistic sign is arbitrary *a priori* but non-arbitrary *a posteriori*. This discussion leads us to keep two different terms, which will be useful during the semiological extension. We shall say that a system is arbitrary when its signs are founded not by convention, but by unilateral decision: the sign is not arbitrary in the language but it is in fashion; and we shall say that a sign is *motivated* when the relation between its signified and its signifier is analogical (Buyssens has put forward, as suitable terms, *intrinsic semes* for motivated signs, and *extrinsic semes* for unmotivated ones). It will therefore be possible to have systems which are arbitrary and motivated, and others which are non-arbitrary and unmotivated.

II.4.3. *The arbitrary and the motivated in semiology:* In linguistics, motivation is limited to the partial plane of derivation or composition; in semiology, on the contrary, it will put to us more general problems. On the one hand, it is possible that outside language systems may be found, in which motivation plays a great part. We shall then have to establish in what way analogy is compatible with the discontinuous character which up to now has seemed necessary to signification; and afterwards how paradigmatic series (that is, in which the terms are few and discrete) can be established when the signifiers are *analoga*: this will probably be the case of 'images', the semiology of which is, for these reasons, far from being established. On the other hand, it is highly probable that a semiological inventory will reveal the existence of impure systems, comprising either very loose motivations, or motivations pervaded, so to speak, with secondary non-motivations, as if, often, the sign lent itself to a kind of conflict between the motivated and the unmotivated. This is already to some extent the case of the most 'motivated' zone of language, that of onomatopoeia. Martinet has pointed out[50] that the onomatopoeic motivation was accompanied by a loss of the double articulation (*ouch*, which depends only on the second articulation, replaces the doubly articulated syntagm '*it hurts*'); yet the onomatopoeia which expresses pain is not exactly the same in French (*aïe*) and in Danish (*au*), for instance. This is because in fact motivation here submits, as it were, to phonological models which of course vary with different languages: there is an impregnation of the analogical by the digital. Outside language, problematic systems, like the 'language' of the bees, show the same ambiguity: the honey-gathering dances have a vaguely analogical value; that at the entrance of the hive is frankly motivated (by the direction of the food), but the wriggly dance in a figure of eight is quite unmotivated (it refers to a distance).[51] Finally, and as a last example of such ill-defined areas,[52] certain trade-marks used in advertising consist of purely 'abstract' (non-analogical) shapes; they can, however, 'express' a certain impression (for instance one of 'power') which has a relation of affinity with the signified. The trade-mark of the Berliet lorries (a circle with a thick arrow across it) does not in any way 'copy' power – indeed, how could one 'copy' power? – and yet suggests it through a latent analogy; the same ambiguity is to be found in the signs of some ideographic writings (Chinese, for instance).

The coexistence of the analogical and the non-analogical therefore seems unquestionable, even within a single system. Yet semiology cannot be content with a description acknowledging this compromise without trying to systematize it, for it cannot admit a continuous differential since, as we shall see, meaning is articulation. These problems have not yet been studied in detail, and it would be impossible to give a general survey of them. The outline of an economy of signification (at the anthropological level) can, however, be perceived: in the language, for instance, the (relative) motivation introduces a certain order at the level of the first (significant) articulation: the 'contract' is therefore in this case underpinned by a certain naturalization of this *a priori* arbitrariness which Lévi-Strauss talks about; other systems, on the contrary, can go from motivation to non-motivation: for instance the set of the ritual puppets of initiation of the Senoufo, cited by Lévi-Strauss in *The Savage Mind*. It is therefore probable that at the level of the most general semiology, which merges with anthropology, there comes into being a sort of circularity between the analogical and the unmotivated: there is a double tendency (each aspect being complementary to the other) to naturalize the unmotivated and to intellectualize the motivated (that is to say, to culturalize it). Finally, some authors are confident that digitalism, which is the rival of the analogical, is itself in its purest form – binarism – a 'reproduction' of certain physiological processes, if it is true that sight and hearing, in the last analysis, function by alternative selections.[53]

II.5. VALUE

II.5.1. *Value in linguistics:* We have said, or at least hinted, that to treat the sign 'in itself', as the only link between signifier and signified, is a fairly arbitrary (although inevitable) abstraction. We must, to conclude, tackle the sign, no longer by way of its 'composition', but of its 'setting': this is the problem of value. Saussure did not see the importance of this notion at the outset, but even as early as his second *Course in General Linguistics*, he increasingly concentrated on it, and value became an essential concept for him, and eventually more important than that of signification (with which it is not co-extensive). Value bears a close relation to the notion of the language (as opposed to speech); its effect is to de-psychologize linguistics and to bring it closer to economics; it is therefore central to structural linguistics. In most sciences, Saussure observes,[54] there is no coexistence of synchrony and diachrony: astronomy is a synchronic science (although the heavenly bodies alter); geology is a diachronic science (although it can study fixed states); history is mainly diachronic (a succession of events), although it can linger over some 'pictures'.[55] Yet there is a science in which these two aspects have an equal share: economics (which include economics proper, and economic history); the same applies to linguistics, Saussure goes on to say. This is because in both cases we are dealing with a system of equivalence between two different things: work and reward, a signifier and a signified (this is the phenomenon which we have up to now called *signification*). Yet, in linguistics as well as in economics, this equivalence is not isolated, for if we alter one of its terms, the whole system changes by degrees. For a sign (or an economic 'value') to exist, it must therefore be possible, on the one hand, to *exchange* dissimilar things (work and wage, signifier and signified), and on the other, to *compare* similar things with each other. One can exchange a five-franc note for bread, soap or a cinema ticket, but one can also compare this banknote with ten- or fifty-franc notes, etc.; in the same way, a 'word' can be 'exchanged' for an idea (that is, for something dissimilar), but it can also be compared with other words (that is, something similar): in English the word *mutton* derives its value only from its coexistence with *sheep*; the meaning is truly fixed only at the end of this double determination: signification and value. Value, therefore, is not signification; it comes, Saussure says,[56] 'from the reciprocal situation of the pieces of the language'. It is even more important than signification: 'what quantity of idea or phonic matter a sign contains is of less import than what there is around it in the other signs':[57] a prophetic sentence, if one realizes that it already was the foundation of Lévi-Strauss's homology and of the principle of taxonomies. Having thus carefully distinguished, with Saussure, signification and value, we immediately see that if we return to Hjelmslev's *strata* (substance and form), the signification partakes of the substance of the content, and value, of that of its form (*mutton* and *sheep* are in a paradigmatic relation *as signifieds* and not, of course, as signifiers).

II.5.2. *The articulation:* In order to account for the double phenomenon of signification and value, Saussure used the analogy of a sheet of paper: if we cut out shapes in it, on the one hand we get various pieces (A, B, C), each of which has a *value* in relation to its neighbours, and, on the other, each of these pieces has a recto and a verso *which have been cut out at the same time* (A—A', B—B', C—C'): this is the signification. This comparison is useful because it leads us to an original conception of the production of meaning: no longer as the mere correlation of a signifier and a signified, but perhaps more essentially *as an act of simultaneously cutting out* two amorphous masses, two 'floating kingdoms' as Saussure says. For Saussure imagines that at the (entirely theoretical) origin of meaning, ideas and sounds form two floating, labile, continuous and parallel masses of substances; meaning intervenes when one cuts at the same time and at a single stroke into these two masses. The signs (thus produced) are therefore *articuli*; meaning is therefore an order with chaos on either side, but this order is essentially a *division*. The language is an intermediate object between sound and thought: it consists *in uniting both while simultaneously decomposing them.* And Saussure suggests a new simile: signifier and signified are like two superimposed layers, one of air, the other of water; when the atmospheric pressure changes, the layer of water divides into waves: in the same way, the signifier is divided into *articuli*. These images, of the sheet of paper as well as of the waves, enable us to emphasize a fact which is of the utmost importance for the future of semiological analysis: that language is the domain of *articulations*, and the meaning is above all a cutting-out of shapes. It follows that the future task of semiology is far less to establish lexicons of objects than to rediscover the articulations which men impose on reality; looking into the distant and perhaps ideal future, we might say that semiology and taxonomy, although they are not yet born, are perhaps meant to be merged into a new science, arthrology, namely, the science of apportionment.

III. SYNTAGM AND SYSTEM

III.1. THE TWO AXES OF LANGUAGE

III.1.1. *Syntagmatic and associative relationships in linguistics:* For Saussure,[58] the relationships between linguistic terms can develop on two planes, each of which generates its own particular values; these two planes correspond to two forms of mental activity (this generalization was to be later adopted by Jakobson). The first plane is that of the *syntagms*; the syntagm is a combination of signs, which has space as a support. In the articulated language, this space is linear and irreversible (it is the 'spoken chain'): two elements cannot be pronounced at the same time (*re-enter, against all, human life*): each term here derives its value from its opposition to what precedes and what follows; in the chain of speech, the terms are really united *in praesentia*; the analytical activity which applies to the syntagm is that of carving out.

The second plane is that of the *associations* (if we still keep Saussure's terminology): 'Beside the discourse (syntagmatic plane), the units which have something in common are associated in memory and thus form groups within which various relationships can be found': *education* can be associated, through its meaning, to *upbringing* or *training*, and through its sound, to *educate, educator*, or to *application, vindication*. Each group forms a potential mnemonic series, a 'mnemonic treasure'; in each series, unlike what happens at the syntagmatic level, the terms are united *in absentia*; the analytic activity which applies to the associations is that of classification.

The syntagmatic and associative planes are united by a close relation, which Saussure has expressed by means of the following simile: each linguistic unit is like a column in a building of antiquity: this column is in a real relation of contiguity with other parts of the building, for instance the architrave (syntagmatic relation); but if this column is Doric, it evokes in us a comparison with other architectural orders, the Ionic or the Corinthian; and this is a potential relation of substitution (associative relation): the two planes are linked in such a way that the syntagm cannot 'progress' except by calling successively on new units taken from the associative plane. Since Saussure, the analysis of the associative plane has undergone considerable development; its very name has changed: we speak today, not of the associative, but of the *paradigmatic* plane,[59] or, as we shall henceforth do here, of the *systematic* plane. The associative plane has evidently a very close connection with 'the language' as a system, while the syntagm is nearer to speech. It is possible to use a subsidiary terminology: syntagmatic connections are *relations* in Hjelmslev, *contiguities* in Jakobson, *contrasts* in Martinet; systematic connections are *correlations* in Hjelmslev, *similarities* in Jakobson, *oppositions* in Martinet.

III.1.2. *Metaphor and Metonymy in Jakobson:* Saussure had an intimation that the syntagmatic and the associative (that is, for us, the systematic) probably corresponded to two forms of mental activity, which meant an excursion outside linguistics. Jakobson, in a now famous text,[60] has adopted this extension by applying the opposition of the *metaphor* (of the systematic order) and the *metonymy* (of the syntagmatic order) to non-linguistic languages: there will therefore be 'discourses' of the metaphorical and of the metonymic types; it is obvious that neither type implies the exclusive use of one of the two models (since both syntagm and system are necessary to all discourse), but only implies the dominance of one of them. To the metaphoric order (in which the associations by substitution predominate) belong (according to Jakobson) the Russian lyrical songs, the works of Romanticism and of Symbolism, Surrealist painting, the films of Charlie Chaplin (in which the superimposed dissolves are equated by Jakobson to veritable filmic metaphors), the Freudian dream-symbols (by identification). To the metonymic order (in which the syntagmatic associations predominate) belong the heroic epics, the narratives of the Realist school, films by Griffith (close-ups, montage, and variations in the angles of the shots) and the oneiric projections by displacement or condensation. To Jakobson's enumeration could be added: on the side of metaphor, didactic expositions (which make use of definitions by substitution),[61] literary criticism of the thematic type, aphoristic types of discourse; on the side of metonymy, popular novels and newspaper narratives.[62] Let us note, following a remark by Jakobson, that the analyst (in the present instance, the semiologist) is better

equipped to speak about metaphor than about metonymy, because the metalanguage in which he must
conduct his analysis is itself metaphorical, and consequently homogeneous with the metaphor which
is its object: and indeed there is an abundant literature on metaphor, but next to nothing on metonymy.

III.1.3. *Semiological prospects:* The vistas Jakobson
opened by his remarks on the predominantly metaphorical and predominantly metonymic types of discourse show us the way towards a passage from
linguistics to semiology. For the two planes of the
articulated language must also exist in other significant systems. Although the units of the syntagm,
which result from a dividing operation, and the lists
of oppositions, which result from a classification, cannot be defined *a priori* but only as the outcome of a
general commutative test of the signifiers and the
signifieds, it is possible to indicate the plane of the
syntagm and that of the system in the case of a few
semiological systems without venturing as yet to
designate the syntagmatic units, or, therefore, the
paradigmatic variations to which they give rise (see
table, page 63). Such are the two axes of language,
and the main part of the semiological analysis consists in distributing the facts which have been listed
on each of these axes. It is logical to begin the work
with the syntagmatic division, since in principle this
is the operation which supplies the units which must
also be classified in paradigms; however, when confronted with an unknown system, it may be more
convenient to start from a few paradigmatic elements
empirically obtained, and to study the system before
the syntagm; but since we are here dealing with

theoretical Elements we shall keep to the logical order, which goes from the syntagm to the system.

III.2. THE SYNTAGM

III.2.1. *Syntagm and speech:* We have seen (I.1.6) that the nature of speech (in the Saussurean sense) was syntagmatic, since quite apart from the amplitude of phonation, it can be defined as a (varied) combination of (recurrent) signs: the spoken sentence is the very type of the syntagm; it is therefore certain that the syntagm has very close similarities to speech. Now for Saussure, there cannot be a linguistics of speech; is the linguistics of the syntagm consequently impossible? Saussure felt the difficulty and was careful to specify in what way the syntagm could not be considered as a speech phenomenon: firstly, because there exist fixed syntagms, which usage forbids us to alter in any way (*So what? Now then!*) and which are out of the reach of the combinative freedom of speech (these stereotyped syntagms therefore become sorts of paradigmatic units); secondly, because the syntagms of speech are constructed according to regular forms which thereby belong to the language (*unget-atable* is constructed after *unattainable, unforgivable,* etc.): there is, therefore, a *form* of the syntagm (in Hjelmslev's sense of the word) dealt with by *syntax* which is, so to speak, the 'glottic' version of the syntagm.[63] This does not alter the fact that the structural 'proximity' of the syntagm and of speech is an important fact: because it ceaselessly offers problems to be analysed, but also – conversely – because it enables a structural explanation to be

	System	*Syntagm*
Garment system	Set of pieces, parts or details which cannot be worn at the same time on the same part of the body, and whose variation corresponds to a change in the meaning of the clothing: toque – bonnet – hood, etc.	Juxtaposition in the same type of dress of different elements: skirt – blouse – jacket.
Food system	Set of foodstuffs which have affinities or differences, within which one chooses a dish in view of a certain meaning: the types of entrée, roast or sweet.	Real sequence of dishes chosen during a meal: this is the menu.
	A restaurant 'menu' actualizes both planes: the horizontal reading of the entrées, for instance, corresponds to the system, the vertical reading of the menu corresponds to the syntagm.	
Furniture system	Set of the 'stylistic' varieties of a single piece of furniture (a bed).	Juxtaposition of the different pieces of furniture in the same space: bed – wardrobe – table, etc.
Architecture system	Variations in style of a single element in a building, various types of roof, balcony, hall, etc.	Sequence of the details at the level of the whole building.

given of certain phenomena of 'naturalization' of connoted discourses. The close relation of syntagm and speech must therefore be kept carefully in mind.

III.2.2. *Discontinuity:* The syntagm presents itself in the form of a 'chain' (the flow of speech, for example). Now as we have seen (II.5.2), meaning can arise only from an articulation, that is, from a simultaneous division of the signifying layer, and the signified mass: language is, as it were, that which *divides* reality (for instance the continuous spectrum of the colours is verbally reduced to a series of discontinuous terms). Any syntagm therefore gives rise to an analytic problem: for it is at the same time continuous and yet cannot be the vehicle of a meaning unless it is articulated. How can we divide the syntagm? This problem arises again with every system of signs: in the articulated language, there have been innumerable discussions on the nature (that is, in fact, on the 'limits') of the word, and for certain semiological systems, we can here foresee important difficulties. True, there are rudimentary systems of strongly discontinuous signs, such as those of the Highway Code, which, for reasons of safety, must be radically different from each other in order to be immediately perceived; but the iconic syntagms, which are founded on a more or less analogical representation of a real scene, are infinitely more difficult to divide, and this is probably the reason for which these systems are almost always duplicated by articulated speech (such as the caption of a photograph) which endows them with the discontinuous aspect which they do not have. In spite of these difficulties, the division of the syntagm is a fundamental operation, since it must yield the paradigmatic units of the system; it is in fact the very definition of the syntagm, to be made of *a substance which must be carved up*.[64] The syntagm, when it takes the form of *speech*, appears as a 'text without end': how can one spot, in this text without end, the significant units, that is, the limits of the signs which constitute it?

III.2.3. *The commutation test:* In linguistics, the dividing up of the 'text without end' is done by means of the commutation test. This operative concept is already found in Trubetzkoy, but it has been established under its present name by Hjelmslev and Udall, at the Fifth Congress of Phonetics in 1936. The commutation test consists of artificially introducing a change in the plane of expression (signifiers) and in observing whether this change brings about a correlative modification on the plane of content (signifieds). The point, in fact, is to create an artificial homology, that is to say a double paradigm, on one point of the 'text without end', in order to check whether the reciprocal substitution of two signifiers has as a consequence *ipso facto* the reciprocal substitution of two signifieds; if the commutation of two signifiers produces a commutation of the signifieds one is assured of having got hold, in the fragment of syntagm submitted to the text, of a syntagmatic unit: the first sign has been cut off from the mass. This operation can naturally be conducted reciprocally in starting from the signifieds: if, for instance, in a Greek substantive, the idea of 'two' is substituted for that of 'several', a change of expression is obtained and the change element is thereby obtained (mark of the dual, and mark of the plural). Certain changes, however, do not bring about any change in the opposite plane: Hjelmslev[65] therefore distinguishes the *commutation*, which generates a change of meaning (*poison/poisson*) from the *substitution*, which changes the expression, and not the content, and vice-versa (*bonjour/bonchour*). We must take note of the fact that the commutation is usually applied first to the plane of the signifiers, since it is the syntagm which has to be divided; one can resort to the signifieds, but this remains purely formal: the signified is not called upon for its own sake, by virtue of its 'substance', but merely as an index of the signifier: it *places* the signifier, that is all. In other words, in the ordinary commutation test, one calls into use the form of the signified (its oppositional value in relation to other signifieds), not its substance: 'The difference between the significations are of use, the significations themselves being without importance' (Belevitch).[66] The commutation test allows us in principle to spot, by degrees, the significant units which together weave the syntagm, thus preparing the classification of those units into paradigms; needless to say, it is possible in linguistics only because the analyst has some knowledge of the meaning of the tongue he analyses. But in semiology, we may come across systems whose meaning is unknown or uncertain: who can be sure that in passing from household bread to fine wheaten bread, or from toque to bonnet, we pass from one signified to another? In most cases, the semiologist will find here the relay of some institutions, some metalanguages, which will supply him with the signifieds which he needs for his commutations: the article on gastronomy or the fashion magazine (here again we find the advantage of non-isological systems);

otherwise, he will have to observe more patiently how consistently certain changes and certain recurrences are produced, like a linguist confronted with an unknown language.

III.2.4. *The syntagmatic units:* The commutation test in principle[67] supplies significant units, that is, fragments of syntagms endowed with a necessary sense; these are still for the time being syntagmatic units, since they are not yet classified: but it is certain that they are already also systematic units, since each one of them is a part of a potential paradigm:

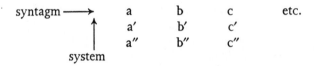

For the time being, we shall observe these units only from the syntagmatic point of view. In linguistics, the commutation test supplies a first type of unit: the *significant units*, each of which is endowed with a signifying facet and a signified facet (the monemes, or, using a more approximate term, the words, themselves compounded of lexemes and morphemes); but by reason of the double articulation of human language, a second commutation test, applied this time to the monemes, produces the appearance of a second type of unit: the *distinctive units* (phonemes).[68] These units have no meaning in themselves, but they nevertheless play their part in the production of meaning, since the commutation of one of them brings about a change of meaning for the moneme it is a part of (the commutation of a voiceless sign into a voiced sign brings about the passage of 'poisson' to 'poison').[69]

In semiology, it is impossible to guess in advance the syntagmatic units which analysis will discover for each system. We shall now be content with anticipating three kinds of problem. The first concerns the existence of complex systems which have combined syntagms as their starting point: a system of objects, like the food or the garment system, can be relayed by a linguistic system proper (the French tongue); we have in this case a garment- or a food-syntagm, and a written syntagm (the spoken chain) *directed towards* them (the dress or the menu recounted by the language): the units of both syntagms do not necessarily coincide: a unit of the food- or the garment-syntagm can be borne by a collection of written units. The second problem arises from the existence, in the semiological systems, of *sign-functions*, namely of signs born from a certain usage and in turn rationalized by it.[70] In opposition to the human language, in which the phonic substance is immediately significant, and only significant, most semiological systems probably involve a matter which has another function beside that of being significant (bread is used to nourish, garments to protect); we can therefore expect that in these systems the syntagmatic unit is composite and includes at least a support for the signification and a variant proper (*long/short skirt*). Finally, it is not out of the question that one might come across systems which are 'scattered', as it were, in which inert spaces of matter support here and there signs which are not only discontinuous but separate: the road-signs of the Highway Code, as found in real life, are separated by long stretches devoid of signification (fragments of roads or streets); one could then speak about syntagms which are (temporarily) dead.[71]

III.2.5 *The combinative constraints:* Once the syntagmatic units are defined for each system, there remains the task of finding the rules which determine their combination and arrangement along the syntagm; the monemes in language, the various garments in a given dress, the dishes in a menu, the road-signs along a street, succeed each other in an order which remains subject to certain constraints: the combination of the signs is free, but this freedom, which is what 'speech' means, remains under supervision (which is why, let it be stated once more, one must not confuse the syntagm with the syntax). In fact, the arrangement is the very condition of the syntagm: 'the syntagm is any set of hetero-functional signs; it is always (at least) binary, and its two terms are in a relation of reciprocal conditioning' (Mikus).[72] Several models of combinative constraints (that is, of the 'logic' of signs) can be imagined; we shall cite here, as examples, the three types of relation which, according to Hjelmslev, two syntagmatic units can enter into when they are contiguous: i) a relation of *solidarity*, when they necessarily imply each other; ii) of *simple implication*, when one implies the other without reciprocity; iii) of *combination*, when neither implies the other. The combinative constraints are fixed by the 'language', but 'speech' complies with them in varying degrees: there remains, therefore, some freedom in the association of syntagmatic units. As far as language is concerned, Jakobson has pointed out that the speaker enjoys, in combining linguistic units, a freedom which increases as he passes from the phoneme to the sentence: the freedom to construct paradigms of phonemes is nil, since the code is here established by the language; the freedom to group phonemes into monemes is limited, for there are 'laws' for governing the creation of words; the freedom to combine several 'words' into a sentence is real, although circumscribed by the syntax and in some cases by submission to certain stereotypes; the freedom to combine sentences is the greatest of all, for it no longer admits of constraints at the level of syntax (the constraints regarding the mental coherence of the discourse are no longer of a linguistic order).

Syntagmatic freedom is clearly related to certain *aleatory factors*: there are probabilities of saturation of certain syntactic forms by certain contents. The verb *to bark* can only be saturated by a reduced number of subjects; within a certain set of clothes, a skirt is unavoidably 'saturated' by a blouse, a sweater or a jacket, etc. This phenomenon is called *catalysis*; it is possible to imagine a purely formal lexicon which would provide, instead of the meaning of each word, the set of other words which could catalyse it according to possibilities which are of course variable – the smallest degree of probability would correspond to a 'poetic' zone of speech (Valle Inclan: 'Woe betide him who does not have the courage to join two words which had never been united').

III.2.6. *Identity and distance of syntagmatic units:* A remark by Saussure suggests that it is because signs recur that language is possible (cf. *supra* I.1.3.) Along the syntagmatic chain we do indeed find a certain number of identical units; the repetition of the signs is, however, corrected by *distance* phenomena between identical units. This problem leads us to statistical linguistics, or macro-linguistics, which is essentially a linguistics of the syntagm, without any reference to meaning. We have seen how near to speech the syntagm was: statistical linguistics is a linguistics of the various forms of speech (Lévi-Strauss). The syntagmatic distance of identical units is not, however, only a problem of macro-linguistics; this distance can be appreciated in stylistic terms (a repetition which occurs too soon being either aesthetically precluded or theoretically recommended) and then becomes an element of the connotative code.

III.3. THE SYSTEM

III.3.1. *Similarity and dissimilarity; difference:* The system constitutes the second axis of the language. Saussure has seen it in the shape of a series of associative fields, some determined by an affinity of sound (*education, saturation*), some by an affinity in meaning (*education, upbringing*). Each field is a store of potential terms (since only one of them is actualized in the present discourse): Saussure insists on the word *term* (he substitutes this for *word*, which is a syntagmatic unit), for, he says, 'as soon as we use "term" instead of "word", the idea of a system is brought to mind.'[73] Indeed, due attention paid to the system in the study of any set of signs practically always testifies to Saussurean influence; the school of Bloomfield, for instance, is reluctant to consider associative relations, while contrary to this, A. Martinet recommends the drawing of a clear distinction between the *contrasts* (relations of contiguity between syntagmatic units) and the *oppositions* (relations between the terms of the associative field).[74] The terms of the field (or paradigm) must at the same time be similar and dissimilar, include a common and a variable element: this is the case on the plane of the signifier, with *education* and *saturation*, and on the plane of the signified with *education* and *upbringing*.

This definition of the terms by means of an opposition seems simple; yet it raises an important theoretical problem. For the element which is common to all the terms of a paradigm (*-ation* in *education* and *saturation*) appears as a positive (non-differential) element, and this phenomenon seems to contradict the reiterated declarations by Saussure on the purely differential, oppositional nature of the language: 'In the language there are only differences without any positive terms'; 'Consider (the sounds) not as sounds having an absolute value, but a purely oppositional, relative, negative, value . . . In stating this, we must go much further, and consider every value in the language as oppositional and not as positive, absolute.'[75] And this, still by Saussure, and even more definite: 'It is a characteristic of the language, as of any semiological system in general, that it can admit no difference between what distinguishes a certain thing and what constitutes that thing.'[76] If, therefore, the language is purely differential, how can it include positive, non-differential elements? In fact, what seems the common element in a paradigm, is itself *elsewhere*, in another paradigm, that is, *according to* *another relevant factor*, a purely differential term: broadly speaking, in the opposition of *le* and *la*, *l* is indeed a common (positive) element, but in *le/ce*, it becomes a differential element: it is therefore relevance which, while limiting Saussure's statement, keeps it true;[77] the meaning still depends on an *aliud/ aliud* relation, which keeps only the difference between two things.[78]

This configuration is questionable, however (whatever Saussure thought), in the semiological systems, in which the matter is not originally significant, and in which, consequently, the units comprise – probably – a positive part (which is the *support* of the signification) and a differential part, the variant; in a *short/long dress*, the vestimentary meaning pervades all the elements (which proves that we are really dealing with a significant unit), but the paradigm never applies to anything but the qualifying element (*long/short*) while the *dress* (support) does keep a positive value. The absolutely differential value of the language is therefore probable only if we mean the articulated language; in the secondary systems (which derive from non-significant usages), the language is 'impure', so to speak: it does contain a differential element (that is, pure 'language') at the level of the variants, but also something positive, at the level of the supports.

III.3.2. *The oppositions:* The internal arrangement of the terms in an associative or paradigmatic field is usually called – at least in linguistics, and more precisely, in phonology – an *opposition*. This is not a very good denomination, for on the one hand it presupposes too much the antonymic character of the paradigmatic relation (Cantineau would have pre-ferred *relation*, and Hjelmslev *correlation*), and on the other hand, it seems to connote a binary relation, about which there is no certainty that it is the foun-dation of all semiological paradigms. We shall, how-ever, keep the word, since it is accepted.

The types of opposition are very varied, as we shall see; but in its relations with the plane of content, an opposition, whatever it may be, always appears as a *homology*, as we have already indicated, apropos of the commutation test: the 'leap' from one term of the opposition to the other accompanies the 'leap' from one signified to the other; it is to respect the differential character of the system that one must always think of the relation between signifier and signified in terms, not simply of analogy, but of at least a four-termed homology.

Besides, the 'leap' from one term to the other is doubly alternating: the opposition between *bière* and *pierre*, although very small (*b/p*), cannot be split into indefinite intermediate states; an approximate sound between *b* and *p* cannot in any way refer to an inter-mediate substance between *beer* and *stone*; there are two parallel leaps: the opposition is still in the *all-or-nothing* category. We again find the principle of difference which is the foundation of opposition: it is this principle which must inspire the analysis of the associative sphere; for to deal with the opposition can only mean to observe the relations of similarity or difference which may exist between the terms of the oppositions, that is, quite precisely, to classify them.

III.3.3. *The classification of oppositions:* We know that since human language is doubly articulated, it comprises two sorts of opposition: the distinctive oppositions (between phonemes), and the significant oppositions (between monemes). Trubetzkoy has suggested a classification of the distinctive oppositions, which J. Cantineau has tried to adopt and extend to the significant oppositions in the language. As at the first glance semiological units are nearer to the semantic units of the language than to its phonological units, we shall give here Cantineau's classification, for even if it cannot be easily applied (subsequently) to the semiological oppositions, it has the advantage of bringing to our notice the main problems posed by the structure of oppositions.[79] At first sight when one passes from a phonological to a semantic system, the oppositions in the latter are innumerable, since each signifier seems to be opposed to all the others; a principle of classification is possible, however, if one chooses as a guide *a typology of the relations between the similar element and the dissimilar element of the opposition.* Thus Cantineau obtains the following types of opposition – which can also be combined with each other.[80]

A. *Oppositions classified according to their relations with the whole of the system*

A.i. *Bilateral and multilateral oppositions.* In these oppositions, the common element between two terms, or 'basis for comparison', is not found in any of the other oppositions of the code (*bilateral oppositions*) or, on the contrary, is found in other oppositions of the code (*multilateral oppositions*). Let us take the written Latin alphabet: the opposition of the figures E/F is bilateral, because the common elt F is not found again in any other letter;[81] on the contrary, the opposition P/R is multilateral, for the P shape (or common element) is again found in B.

A.2. *Proportional and isolated oppositions.* In these oppositions, the difference is constituted into a sort of model. Thus: *Mann/Männer* and *Land/Länder* are proportional oppositions; in the same way: (*nous*) *disons/(vous) dites* and (*nous*) *faisons/(vous) faites*. The oppositions which are not proportional are isolated; they are evidently the most numerous. In semantics, only grammatical (morphological) oppositions are proportional; the lexical oppositions are isolated.

B. *Oppositions classified according to the relation between the terms of the oppositions*

B.1. *Privative oppositions.* These are the best known. A privative opposition means any opposition in which the signifier of a term is characterized by the presence of a significant element, or *mark*, which is missing in the signifier of the other. This is therefore the general opposition *marked/unmarked: mange* (without any indication of the person or number): unmarked term; *mangeons* (first person of the plural): marked term. This disposition corresponds in logic to the relation of inclusion. We shall mention in this connection two important problems. The first concerns the *mark*. Some linguists have identified the mark with the exceptional and have invoked a feeling for the normal in order to decide which terms are *unmarked*; according to them, the *unmarked* is what is frequent or banal, or else derived from the *marked* by a subsequent subtraction. Thus is reached

the idea of a negative mark (that which is subtracted) :
for the unmarked terms are more numerous in the
language than the marked ones (Trubetzkoy, Zipf).
Thus Cantineau considers that *rond* is marked, in relation to *ronde*, which is not; but this is in fact because Cantineau appeals to the content, according to
which the masculine is marked in relation to the
feminine. For Martinet, on the contrary, the mark is
literally an *additional* significant element; this does
not prevent in any way, in the case of *masculine/*
feminine, the parallelism which normally exists between the mark of the signifier and that of the
signified, for 'masculine' in fact corresponds to a non-
differentiation between the sexes, to a kind of
abstract generality (il fait *beau*, on est *venu*), as opposed to which, the feminine is well marked; a
semantic mark and a formal mark go well together :
when one wants to say more, one adds a supple-
mentary sign.[82]

The second problem arising in connection with
privative opposition is that of the unmarked term.
It is called the *zero degree* of the opposition. The zero
degree is therefore not a total absence (this is a
common mistake), *it is a significant absence*. We have
here a pure differential state; the zero degree testifies
to the power held by any system of signs, of creating
meaning 'out of nothing': 'the language can be content with an opposition of something and nothing.'[83]
The concept of the zero degree, which sprang from
phonology, lends itself to a great many applications :
in semantics, in which *zero signs* are known ('a "zero
sign" is spoken of in cases where the absence of any
explicit signifier functions by itself as a signifier');[84]
in logic ('A is in the zero state, that is to say that A

77

does not actually exist, but under certain conditions it can be made to appear');[85] in ethnology, where Lévi-Strauss could compare the notion of mana to it ('. . . the proper function of the zero phoneme is to be opposed to the absence of the phoneme . . . Similarly, it could be said . . . that the function of notions of the "mana" type is to be opposed to the absence of signification without involving in itself any particular signification');[86] finally, in rhetoric, where, carried on to the connotative plane, the absence of rhetorical signifiers constitutes in its turn a stylistic signifier.[87]

B.2. *Equipollent oppositions.* In these oppositions, whose relation would in logic be a relation of exteriority, the two terms are equivalent, that is to say that they cannot be considered as the negation and the affirmation of a peculiarity (privative oppositions): in *foot/feet*, there is neither mark nor absence of mark. These oppositions are semantically the most numerous, even if the language, for economy's sake, often attempts to replace equipollent oppositions by privative oppositions: first, because in the latter the relation between similarity and dissimilarity is well balanced, and second, because they enable us to build proportional series such as *poet/poetess, count/countess*, etc., whereas *stallion/mare*, which is an equipollent opposition, has no derivation.[88]

C. *Oppositions classified according to the extent of their differentiating value*

C.1. *Constant oppositions.* This is the case of the signifieds which *always* have different signifiers: (*je*) *mange*/(*nous*) *mangeons*; the first person of the singular and that of the plural have different signifiers, in French, in all verbs, tenses and modes.

C.2. *Oppositions which can be eliminated or neutralized*. This is the case of the signifieds which do not always have different signifiers, so that the two terms of the opposition can sometimes be identical: to the semantic opposition *third person singular/third person plural*, there correspond signifiers which are at one time different (*finit/finissent*), at others phonetically identical (*mange/mangent*).

III.3.4. *Semiological oppositions:* What may become of these types of opposition in semiology? It is naturally much too early to tell, for the paradigmatic plane of a new system cannot be analysed without a broad inventory. Nothing proves that the types laid down by Trubetzkoy and partly[89] adopted by Cantineau could concern systems other than language: new types of opposition are conceivable, especially if one is prepared to depart from the binary model. We shall, however, attempt to sketch here a confrontation between the types of Trubetzkoy and Cantineau and what can be known about two very different semiological systems: the Highway Code and the fashion system.

In the Highway Code we shall find multilateral proportional oppositions (for instance, all those which are built on a variation of colour within the opposition of circle and triangle), private oppositions (when an added mark makes the meaning of a circle vary, for instance) and constant oppositions (the signifieds always have different signifiers), but neither equipollent nor suppressible oppositions. This economy is

79

understandable: the Highway Code must be immediately and unambiguously legible if it is to prevent accidents; therefore it eliminates those oppositions which need the longest time to be understood, either because they are not reducible to proper paradigms (equipollent oppositions) or because they offer a choice of two signifieds for a single signifier (suppressible oppositions).

On the contrary, in the fashion system,[90] which tends to polysemy, we encounter all types of opposition, except, of course, bilateral and constant oppositions, whose effect would be to increase the particularity and the rigidity of the system.

Semiology, in the proper sense of the word, that is, as a science comprising all systems of signs, will therefore be able to make good use of the general distribution of the types of opposition throughout the various systems – an observation which would have no object at the level of the language only. But above all, the extension of semiological research will probably lead to the study (which may eventually prove fruitless) of serial, and not only oppositional, paradigmatic relations; for it is not certain that, once confronted with complex objects, deeply involved in some matter and in various usages, one will be able to reduce the functioning of the meaning to the alternative of two polar elements or to the opposition of a mark and a zero degree. This leads us to remind the reader once more that the most vexed question connected with paradigms is that of the binary principle.

III.3.5. *Binarism:* The importance and the simplicity of the privative opposition (*marked/unmarked*), which is by definition an alternative, have led to the question whether all known oppositions should not be reduced to the binary pattern (that is, based on the presence or absence of a mark), in other words, whether the binary principle did not reflect a universal fact; and on the other hand, whether, being universal, it might not have a natural foundation.

About the first point, it is certain that binary patterns are very frequently encountered. It is a principle which has been acknowledged for centuries, that information can be transmitted by means of a binary code, and most of the artificial codes which have been invented by very different societies have been binary, from the 'bush telegraph' (and notably the *talking drum* of the Congo tribes, which has two notes) to the morse alphabet and the contemporary developments of 'digitalism', or alternative codes with 'digits' in computers and cybernetics. However, if we leave the plane of the 'logo-techniques', to come back to that of the systems which are not artificial, which concerns us here, the universality of the binary principle appears far less certain. Paradoxically, Saussure himself never did conceive the associative field as binary: for him, the terms of a field are neither finite in number, nor determined in their order: [91] 'A term is like the centre of a constellation, the point where other co-ordinate terms, the sum of which is indefinite, converge.' [92] The only restriction imposed by Saussure concerns the flexional paradigms, which of course are finite series. It is phonology which has focused attention on the binarism of language (only at the level of the second articulation, it is true); is this binarism absolute? Jakobson thinks so: [93] according to him, the phonetic systems of all languages could be described by means of a dozen distinctive features,

81

all of them binary, that is to say, either present or absent, or, as the case may be, irrelevant. This binary universalism has been questioned and qualified by Martinet:[94] binary oppositions are the majority, not the totality; the universality of binarism is not certain. Questioned in phonology, unexplored in semantics, binarism is the great unknown in semiology, whose types of opposition have not yet been outlined. To account for complex oppositions, one can of course resort to the model brought to light by linguistics, and which consists in a 'complicated' alternative, or four-termed opposition: two polarized terms (*this or that*), a mixed term (*this and that*) and a neutral term (*neither this nor that*); these oppositions, although they are more flexible than the privative oppositions, will probably not save us from having to pose the problem of the *serial*, and not only oppositive, paradigms: the universality of binarism is not yet founded.

Nor is its 'naturalness' (and this is the second point in which it lays itself open to discussion). It is very tempting to found the general binarism of the codes on physiological data, inasmuch as it is likely that neuro-cerebral perception also functions in an all-or-nothing way, and particularly sight and hearing, which seem to work by means of a review of alternatives.[95] Thus would be elaborated, from nature to society, a vast, 'digital', not 'analogical', translation of the world; but nothing of all this is certain. In fact, and to conclude briefly on the question of binarism, we may wonder whether this is not a classification which is both necessary and transitory: in which case binarism also would be a metalanguage, a particular taxonomy meant to be swept away by history, after having been true to it for a moment.

III.3.6. *Neutralization:* In order to finish with the principal phenomena pertaining to the system, a word has to be said about *neutralization*. This term means in linguistics the phenomenon whereby a relevant opposition loses its relevance, that is, ceases to be significant. In general, the neutralization of a systematic opposition occurs in response to the context: it is therefore the syntagm which cancels out the system, so to speak. In phonology, for instance, the opposition between two phonemes can be nullified as a consequence of the position of one of the terms in the spoken chain: in French, there is normally an opposition between *é* and *è* when one of these terms is at the end of a word (*j'aimai/j'aimais*); this opposition ceases to be relevant anywhere else: it is neutralized. Conversely, the relevant opposition *ó/ò* (*saute/sotte*) is neutralized at the end of a word, where one finds only the sound *ó* (*pot, mot, eau*). In this case the two neutralized features are reunited under a single sound which is called *archiphoneme*, and which is written with a capital letter: *é/è*=E; *ó/ò*=O.

In semantics, neutralization has been the object of only a few soundings since the semantic 'system' is not yet established: J. Dubois[98] has observed that a semantic unit can lose its relevant features in certain syntagms; around 1872, in phrases such as: *emancipation of the workers, emancipation of the masses, emancipation of the proletariat*, both parts of the phrase can be commuted without altering the meaning of the complex semiology unit.

In semiology, we must once more wait for a certain number of systems to be reconstructed before outlining a theory of neutralization. Some systems will

perhaps radically exclude the phenomenon: by reason
of its very purpose, which is the immediate and unambiguous understanding of a small number of signs,
the Highway Code cannot tolerate any neutralization. Fashion, on the contrary, which has polysemic
(and even pansemic) tendencies, admits numerous
neutralizations: whereas in one case *chandail* refers
back to the seaside, and *sweater* to the mountains, in
another case it will be possible to speak of a *chandail
ou un sweater* for the seaside; the relevance *chandail/
sweater* is lost:[97] the two pieces are absorbed into
a kind of 'archi-vesteme' of the 'woollen' type. We
may say, at least as far as the semiological hypothesis
is concerned (that is, when we disregard the problems
raised by the second articulation, that of the purely
distinctive units), that there is a neutralization when
two signifiers fall under the heading of a single signified, or vice-versa (for it will also be possible for the
signifieds to be neutralized).

Two useful notions must be mentioned in connection with this phenomenon. The first is that of the
field of dispersal or *security margin*. The dispersal
field is made up of the varieties in execution of a
unit (of a phoneme, for instance) as long as these
varieties do not result in an alteration in meaning
(that is, as long as they do not become relevant variations); the 'edges' of the dispersal field are its margins
of security. This is a notion which is not very useful
in dealing with a system in which the 'language' is
very strong (in the car system, for instance), but valu-
able when a rich 'speech' multiplies the opportunities
for difference in execution: in the food system, for
instance, we can speak of the dispersal field of a

dish, which will be established by the limits within which this dish remains significant, whatever 'frills' the performer brings into its preparation.

Here is the second notion: the varieties which make up the dispersal field are sometimes called *combinative variants* when they depend on the combination of signs, that is, on the immediate context (the *d* of *nada* and that of *fonda* are not identical, but the variation does not affect the meaning), sometimes *individual* or *optional* variants. In French, for instance, whether you are a native of Burgundy or Paris, that is to say whether you use a rolled or uvular *r*, you are understood just the same. The combinative variants have long been considered as phenomena pertaining to speech; they certainly are very close to it, but are nowadays held to pertain to the language, since they are 'compulsory'. It is probable that in semiology, where studies on connotation are likely to be important, the combinative variations will become a central notion: for variants which are non-significant on the plane of denotation (for instance the rolled and the uvular *r*) can become significant on the plane of connotation, and from being combinative variants they refer now to two different signifieds: in the language of the theatre, one will signify 'the Burgundian', the other 'the Parisian', without ceasing to be non-significant in the denotative system.

Such are the first implications of neutralization. In a very general way, neutralization represents a sort of pressure of the syntagm on the system, and we know that the syntagm, which is close to speech, is to a certain extent a factor of 'defaulting'; the strongest systems (like the Highway Code) have poor syntagms; the great syntagmatic complexes (like the image system) tend to make the meaning ambiguous.

III.3.7. *Transgressions:* Syntagm system : such are the two planes of language. Now, although such studies are only to be found here and there in a sketchy way, we must foresee the future exhaustive exploration of the whole of the phenomena in which one plane overlaps the other, in a way which is 'teratological', so to speak, compared to the normal relations of the system and the syntagm. For the mode of articulation of the two axes is sometimes 'perverted', when for instance a paradigm is extended into a syntagm. There is then a defiance of the usual distribution *syntagm/system*, and it is probably around this transgression that a great number of creative phenomena are situated, as if perhaps there were here a junction between the field of aesthetics and the defections from the semantic system. The chief transgression is obviously the extension of a paradigm on to the syntagmatic plane, since normally only one term of the operation is actualized, the other (or others) remaining potential : this is what would happen, broadly speaking, if one attempted to elaborate a discourse by putting one after the other all the terms of the same declension. The question of these syntagmatic extensions had already arisen in phonology, where Trnka, corrected in many respects by Trubetzkoy, had posited that within a morpheme, two paradigmatic terms of a correlative couple cannot occur side by side.

But it is evidently in semantics that normality (to which Trnka's law refers in phonology) and the departures from it have the greatest interest, since we are there on the plane of significant (and no longer distinctive) units, and since the overlapping of the axes of language brings about an apparent alteration in the meaning. Here are, from this point of view, three directions which will have to be explored.

In face of the classical oppositions or oppositions of *presence*, J. Tubiana[98] suggests the acknowledgment of oppositions of *arrangement*: two words exhibit the same features, but the arrangement of these features differs in both: *rame/mare*; *dur/rude*; *charme/marche*. These oppositions form the majority of plays on words, puns and spoonerisms. In fact, starting from a relevant opposition, (*Félibres/fébriles*), it is sufficient to remove the stroke which indicates the paradigmatic opposition to obtain a strange-sounding syntagm (a newspaper has in fact used *Félibres fébriles* as a title); this sudden suppression of the stroke is rather reminiscent of the removal of a kind of structural censorship, and one cannot fail to connect this phenomenon with that of dreams as producers or explorers of puns.[99]

Another direction which has to be explored, and an important one, is that of rhyme. Rhyming produces an associative sphere at the level of sound, that is to say, of the signifiers: there are paradigms of rhymes. In relation to these paradigms, the rhymed discourse is clearly made of a fragment of the system extended into a syntagm. According to this, rhyming coincides with a transgression of the law of the distance between the syntagm and the system (Trnka's law); it corresponds to a deliberately created tension between the congenial and the dissimilar, to a kind of structural scandal.

Finally, rhetoric as a whole will no doubt prove to

87

be the domain of these creative transgressions; if we remember Jakobson's distinction, we shall understand that any metaphoric series is a syntagmatized paradigm, and any metonymy a syntagm which is frozen and absorbed in a system; in metaphor, selection becomes contiguity, and in metonymy, contiguity becomes a field to select from. It therefore seems that it is always on the frontiers of the two planes that creation has a chance to occur.

IV. DENOTATION AND
CONNOTATION

IV.I. STAGGERED SYSTEMS

It will be remembered that any system of significations comprises a plane of expression (E) and a plane of content (C) and that the signification coincides with the relation (R) of the two planes: E R C. Let us now suppose that such a system E R C becomes in its turn a mere element of a second system, which thus is more extensive than the first: we then deal with two systems of significations which are imbricated but are out of joint with each other, or staggered. But this derivation can occur in two entirely different ways dependent upon the point of insertion of the first system into the second, and therefore it can result in two opposite sets.

In the first case, *the first system (ERC) becomes the plane of expression, or signifier, of the second system:*

2	E	R	C
I	E R C		

or else: (ERC) RC. This is the case which Hjelmslev calls *connotative semiotics*; the first system is then the plane of *denotation* and the second system (wider than the first) the plane of *connotation*. We shall therefore say that *a connoted system is a system whose plane of expression is itself constituted by a signifying system:* the common cases of connotation will of course consist of complex systems of which language forms the first system (this is, for instance, the case with literature).

In the second (opposite) case of derivation, *the first system (ERC) becomes, not the plane of expression, as in connotation, but the plane of content, or signified, of the second system=*

$$
\begin{array}{cccc}
2 & E & R & \overset{\frown}{C} \\
1 & & & \overline{E\,R\,C}
\end{array}
$$

or else: E R (ERC). This is the case with all *metalanguages: a metalanguage is a system whose plane of content is itself constituted by a signifying system; or else, it is a semiotics which treats of a semiotics.*

Such are the two ways of amplification of double systems:

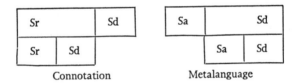

Connotation   Metalanguage

IV.2. CONNOTATION

Connotative phenomena have not yet been systematically studied (a few indications will be found in Hjelmslev's *Prolegomena*). Yet the future probably belongs to a linguistics of connotation, for society continually develops, from the first system which human language supplies to it, second-order significant systems, and this elaboration, now proclaimed and now disguised, is very close to a real historical anthropolgy. Connotation, being itself a system, comprises signifiers, signifieds, and the process which unites the former to the latter (signification), and it is the inventory of these three elements which one should undertake in the first place for each system.

The signifiers of connotation, which we shall call *connotators*, are made up of *signs* (signifiers and signifieds united) of the denoted system. Naturally, several denoted signs can be grouped together to form a single connotator – provided the latter has a single signified of connotation; in other words, the units of the connoted system do not necessarily have the same size as those of the denoted system: large fragments of the denoted discourse can constitute a single unit of the connoted system (this is the case, for instance, with the tone of a text, which is made up of numerous words, but which nevertheless refers to a single signified). Whatever the manner in which it 'caps' the denoted message, connotation does not exhaust it: there always remains 'something denoted' (otherwise the discourse would not be possible) and the connotators are always in the last analysis discontinuous and scattered signs, naturalized by the denoted language which carries them.

As for the signified of connotation, its character is at once general, global and diffuse; it is, if you like, a fragment of ideology: the sum of the messages in French refers, for instance, to the signified 'French'; a book can refer to the signified 'Literature'. These signifieds have a very close communication with culture, knowledge, history, and it is through them, so to speak, that the environmental world invades the system. We might say that *ideology* is the *form* (in Hjelmslev's sense of the word) of the signifieds of connotation, while *rhetoric* is the form of the connotators.

IV.3. METALANGUAGE

In connotative semiotics, the signifiers of the second system are constituted by the signs of the first; this is reversed in metalanguage : there the signifieds of the second system are constituted by the signs of the first. Hjelmslev has made the notion of metalanguage explicit in the following way : it being understood that an *operation* is a *description* founded on the empirical principle, that is to say non-contradictory (coherent), exhaustive and simple, scientific semiotics, or metalanguage, is an operation, whereas connotative semiotics is not. It is evident that semiology, for instance, is a metalanguage, since as a second-order system it takes over a first language (or language-object) which is the system under scrutiny; and this system-object is *signified* through the metalanguage of semiology. The notion of metalanguage must not be confined to scientific languages; when ordinary language, *in its denoted state*, takes over a system of signifying objects, it becomes an 'operation', that is, a metalanguage. This is the case, for instance, with the fashion magazine which 'speaks' the significations of garments, just as one speaks a language; this, however, is only ideally speaking, for magazines do not usually exhibit a purely denoted discourse, so that eventually we deal here with a complex ensemble, where language, at its denoted level, is a metalanguage, but where this metalanguage is in its turn caught up in a process of connotation:

3 Connotation	Sr : rhetoric	Sd = ideology
2 Denotation: Metalanguage	Sd	
1 Real System	Sr Sd	

IV.4. CONNOTATION AND METALANGUAGE

Nothing in principle prevents a metalanguage from becoming in its turn the language-object of a new metalanguage; this would, for example, be the case with semiology if it were to be 'spoken' by another science. If one agreed to define the social sciences as coherent, exhaustive and simple languages (Hjelmslev's empirical principle), that is as *operations*, each new science would then appear as a new language which would have as its object the metalanguage which precedes it, while being directed towards the reality-object which is at the root of these 'descriptions'; the history of the social sciences would thus be, in a sense, a diachrony of metalanguages, and each science, including of course semiology, would contain the seeds of its own death, in the shape of the language destined to speak it. This relativity, which is an inherent part of the general system of metalanguages, allows us to qualify the image which we might at first form, of a semiologist over-confident in the face of connotation; the whole of a semiological analysis usually requires, in addition to the studied system and the (denoted) language which in most cases takes it over, a system of connotation and the metalanguage of the analysis which is applied to it. We might say that society, which holds the plane of connotation, speaks the signifiers of the system considered, while the semiologist speaks its signifieds; he therefore seems to have the objective function of decipherer (his language is an operation) in relation to the world which naturalizes or conceals the signs of the first system under the signifiers of the second; but his objectivity is made provisional by the very history which renews metalanguages.

The aim of semiological research is to reconstitute
the functioning of the systems of significations other
than language in accordance with the process typical
of any structuralist activity, which is to build a
simulacrum of the objects under observation.[100] To
undertake this research, it is necessary frankly to
accept from the beginning (and especially at the beginning) a limiting principle. This principle, which
once more we owe to linguistics, is the principle of
relevance:[101] it is decided to describe the facts which
have been gathered *from one point of view only*, and
consequently to keep, from the heterogeneous mass
of these facts, only the features associated with this
point of view, to the exclusion of any others (these
features are said to be *relevant*). The phonologist, for
instance, examines sounds only from the point of
view of the meaning which they produce without
concerning himself with their physical, articulated
nature; the relevance chosen by semiological research
centres by definition round the signification of the
objects analysed: these are examined only in relation to the meaning which is theirs, without bringing in – at least prematurely, that is, before the
system is reconstituted as far as possible – the other
determining factors of these objects (whether psycho-
logical, sociological or physical). These other factors

must of course not be denied – they each are ascrib-able to another type of relevance; but they must them-selves be treated in semiological terms, that is to say that their place and their function in the system of meaning must be determined. Fashion, for instance, evidently has economic and sociological implications; but the semiologist will treat neither the economics nor the sociology of fashion : he will only say at which level of the semantic system of fashion economics and sociology acquire semiological relevance : at the level of the vestmentary sign, for instance, or at that of the associative constraints (taboos), or at that of the discourse of connotation.

The principle of relevance evidently has as a con-sequence for the analyst a situation of *immanence* : one observes a given system *from the inside*. Since, however, the limits of the system which is the object of the research are not known in advance (the object being precisely to reconstitute this system), the *im-manence* can only apply at the beginning to a hetero-geneous set of facts which will have to be processed for their structure to be known : this is the *corpus*. The corpus is a finite collection of materials, which is determined in advance by the analyst, with some (inevitable) arbitrariness, and on which he is going to work. For instance, if one wishes to reconstitute the food system of the French of today, one will have to decide in advance which body of documents the analysis will deal with (menus found in magazines? restaurant menus? menus observed in real life? menus passed on by word of mouth?), and once this corpus has been defined, one will have to keep to it : that is to say, on the one hand not add anything to it during the course of the research, but also exhaust it completely by analysis, every fact included in the corpus having to be found in the system.

How should one choose the corpus on which one is going to work? This obviously depends on the suspected nature of the system: a corpus of facts concerning food cannot be submitted to the same criteria of choice as a corpus of car models. We can only venture here two general recommendations.

First, the corpus must be wide enough to give reasonable hope that its elements will saturate a complete system of resemblances and differences; it is certain that when one goes through a collection of data, after a time one eventually comes across facts and relations which have already been noticed (we have seen that an identity of signs is a phenomenon pertaining to the language); these 'returns' are more and more frequent, until one no longer discovers any new material: the corpus is then saturated.

Second, the corpus must be as homogeneous as possible. To begin with, homogeneous in substance: there is an obvious interest in working on materials constituted by one and the same substance, like the linguist who deals only with the phonic substance; in the same way, ideally, a good corpus of documents on the food system should comprise only one and the same type of document (restaurant menus, for instance). Reality, however, most commonly presents mixed substances; for instance, garments and written language in fashion; images, music and speech in films, etc; it will therefore be necessary to accept heterogeneous corpuses, but to see to it, in that case, that one makes a careful study of the systematic articulation of the substances concerned (and chiefly, that one

97

pays due attention to separating the real from the language which takes it over), that is, that one gives to their very heterogeneity a structural interpretation.

Further, homogeneous in time: in principle, the corpus must eliminate diachronic elements to the utmost; it must coincide with a state of the system, a cross-section of history. Without here entering into the theoretical debate between synchrony and diachrony, we shall only say that, from an operative point of view, the corpus must keep as close as possible to the synchronic sets. A varied but temporally limited corpus will therefore be preferable to a narrow corpus stretched over a length of time, and if one studies press phenomena, for instance, a sample of newspapers which appeared at the same time will be preferable to the run of a single paper over several years. Some systems establish their own synchrony of their own accord – fashion, for instance, which changes every year; but for the others one must choose a short period of time, even if one has to complete one's research by taking soundings in the diachrony. These initial choices are purely operative and inevitably in part arbitrary: it is impossible to guess the speed at which systems will alter, since the essential aim of semiological research (that is, what will be found last of all) may be precisely to discover the systems' own particular time, the history of forms.

NOTES

[1] 'A concept is assuredly not a thing, but neither is it merely the consciousness of a concept. A concept is an instrument and a history, that is, a bundle of possibilities and obstacles involved in the world as experienced.' (G. G. Granger, *Méthodologie économique*, p. 23.)

[2] A danger stressed by C. Lévi-Strauss, *Anthropologie structurale*, p. 58. *Structural Anthropology*, tr. by Claire Jacobson and Brooke Grundfest Schoepf (Basic Books, New York and London, 1963), pp. 47–8.

[3] This feature has been noted (with misgiving) by M. Cohen ('Linguistique moderne et idéalisme', in *Recherches internationales*, May 1958, no. 7).

[4] It should be noted that the first definition of the language (*langue*) is taxonomic: it is a principle of classification.

[5] Cf. *infra*, II.5.1.

[6] *Acta linguistica*, I, 1, p. 5.

[7] L. Hjelmslev: *Essais Linguistiques* (Copenhagen, 1959), pp. 69 ff.

[8] Cf. *infra*, II.1.3.

[9] Cf. *infra*, II.1.3.

[10] 'La mécanique de l'analyse quantitative en linguistique', in *Études de linguistique appliquée*, 2, Didier, p. 37.

[11] A. Martinet: *Éléments de linguistique générale* (Armand Colin, 1960), p. 30. *Elements of General Linguistics*, tr. by Elizabeth Palmer (Faber & Faber, 1964), pp. 33–4.

[12] Cf. *infra* on the syntagm, Ch. III.

[13] Saussure, in R. Godel, *Les sources manuscrites du Cours de Linguistique générale* (Droz, Minard, 1957), p. 90.

[14] Cf. *infra*, Ch. IV.

[15] R. Jakobson, 'Deux aspects du langage et deux types d'aphasies', in *Essais de Linguistique générale* (Éditions de Minuit), 1963, p. 54. This is the second part of *Fundamentals of Language* (R. Jakobson and M. Halle, The Hague, 1956). C. L. Ebeling, *Linguistic units* (Mouton, The Hague, 1960), p. 9.

A. Martinet, *A functional view of language* (Oxford, Clarendon Press, 1962), p. 105.

[16] *Writing Degree Zero.*

[17] *Essais de Linguistique générale*, Chapter 9. This is a translation of *Shifters, verbal categories and the Russian verb* (Russian Language Project, Department of Slavic Languages and Literature, Harvard University, 1957).

[18] W. Doroszewski, 'Langue et Parole', *Odbitka z Prac Filogisznych*, XLV (Warsaw, 1930), pp. 485–97.

[19] M. Merleau-Ponty, *Phénoménologie de la Perception*, 1945, p. 229. *Phenomenology of Perception*, tr. by Colin Smith. (Routledge & Kegan Paul, in conjunction with the Humanities Press, New York, 1962), pp. 196–7.

[20] M. Merleau-Ponty, *Eloge de la Philosophie* (Gallimard, 1953).

[21] G. Granger, 'Evènement et structure dans les sciences de l'homme', in *Cahiers de l'Institut de science économique appliquée*, no. 55, May 1957.

[22] See F. Braudel, 'Histoire et sciences sociales: la longue durée', in *Annales*, Oct.–Dec. 1958.

[23] *Anthropologie Structurale*, p. 230 (*Structural Anthropology*, pp. 208–9), and 'Les mathématiques de l'homme', in *Esprit*, Oct. 1956.

[24] 'There never is any premeditation, or even any meditation, or reflection on forms, outside the act, the occasion of speech, except an unconscious, non-creative activity: that of classifying' (Saussure, in Godel, op. cit., p. 58).

[25] *Principes de Phonologie* (tr. by J. Cantineau, 1957 ed.). p. 19.

[26] Cf. *infra*, Ch. IV.

[27] Cf. *infra*, II.4.3.

[28] J. P. Charlier: 'La notion de signe (σημεῖον) dans le IVè évangile', in *Revue des sciences philosophiques et théologiques*, 1959, 43, no. 3, pp. 434–48.

[29] This was very clearly expressed by St Augustine: 'A sign is something which, in addition to the substance absorbed by the senses, calls to mind of itself some other thing'.

[30] Cf. the shifters and the indicial symbols, *supra*, I.1.8.

[31] H. Wallon, *De l'acte à la pensée*, 1942, pp. 175–250.

[32] Although very rudimentary, the analysis given here, *supra*, II.1.1, concerns the *form* of the following signifieds: sign, symbol, index, signal.

[33] The case of the pictorial image should be set aside, for the image is immediately communicative, if not significant.

[34] Cf. R. Barthes: 'A propos de deux ouvrages récents de Cl. Lévi-Strauss: Sociologie et Socio-Logique', in *Information sur les sciences sociales* (UNESCO), Vol. 1, no. 4, Dec. 1962, pp. 114–22.

[35] Cf. *infra*, II.4.2.

[36] This discussion was taken up again by Borgeaud, Bröcker and Lohmann, in *Acta linguistica*, III.1.27.

[37] R. Hallig and W. von Wartburg, *Begriffssystem als Grundlage für die Lexicographie* (Berlin, Akademie Verlag, 1952), XXV.

[38] The bibliography of Trier and Matoré will be found in P. Guiraud, *La Sémantique*, P.U.F. ('Que sais-je?'), pp. 70 ff.

[39] This is what we have attempted to do here for *sign* and *symbol* (*supra*, II.1.1.).

[40] These examples are given by G. Mounin: 'Les analyses sémantiques', in *Cahiers de l'Institut de science économique appliquée*, March 1962, no. 123.

[41] It would be advisable henceforth to adopt the distinction suggested by A. J. Greimas: *semantic* = referring to the content; *semiological* = referring to the expression.

[42] Cf. R. Francès, *La perception de la musique* (Vrin, 1958), 3rd part.

[43] Cf. *infra*, III.2.3.

[44] Cf. *infra*, Ch. *III* (Syntagm and system).

[45] Cf. *infra*, II.5.2.

[46] Cf. R. Ortigues, *Le discours et le symbole* (Aubier, 1962).

[47] Cf. *infra*, Ch. IV.

[48] J. Laplanche et S. Leclaire, 'L'inconscient', in *Temps Modernes*, no. 183, July 1963, pp. 81 ff.

[49] E. Benveniste, 'Nature du signe linguistique', in *Acta linguistica*, I, 1939.

[50] A. Martinet, *Economie des changements phonétiques* (Francke, 1955), 5, 6.

[51] Cf. G. Mounin, 'Communication linguistique humaine et communication non-linguistique animale', in *Temps Modernes*, April–May 1960.

[52] Another example would be the Highway Code.

[53] Cf. *infra*, III.3.5.

[54] Saussure, *Cours de Linguistique Générale*, p. 115. *Course in General Linguistics*, tr. by W. Baskin (New York Library and Peter Owen, London, 1950), pp. 79–80.

[55] We may recall that since Saussure's day, History too has discovered the importance of synchronic strutures. Economics,

linguistics, ethnology and history constitute today a *quadrivium* of pilot sciences.

[56] Saussure, in R. Godel, op. cit., p. 90.

[57] Ibid., p. 166. It is obvious that Saussure was thinking of the comparison of the signs not on the plane of syntagmatic succession, but on that of the potential paradigmatic reserves, or associative fields.

[58] Saussure, *Cours de Linguistique Générale*, pp. 170 ff. *Course in General Linguistics*, pp. 122 ff.

[59] Paradeigma: model, table of the flexions of a word given as model, declension.

[60] R. Jakobson, 'Deux aspects du langage et deux types d'aphasie', in *Temps Modernes*, no. 188, Jan. 1962, pp. 853 ff., reprinted in *Essais de Linguistique générale* (Editions de Minuit, 1963), Ch. 2.

[61] This is only a very general polarization, for in fact metaphor and definition cannot be confused (cf. R. Jakobson, *Essais* ... , p. 220).

[62] Cf. R. Barthes, 'L'imagination du signe', in *Essais Critiques* (Seuil, 1964).

[63] 'Glottic': which belongs to the language – as opposed to speech.

[64] B. Mandelbrot has very rightly compared the evolution of linguistics to that of the theory of gases, *from the standpoint of discontinuity* ('Linguistique statistique macroscopique', in *Logigue, Langage et Théorie de l'Information* (P.U.F., 1957)).

[65] L. Hjelmslev, *Essais linguistiques*, p. 103.

[66] *Langage des machines et langage humain*, Hermann, 1956, p. 91.

[67] In principle, for we must set aside the case of the distinctive units of the second articulation, cf. *infra*, same paragraph.

[68] Cf. *supra*, II.1.2.

[69] The problem of the syntagmatic segmentation of the significant units has been tackled in a new fashion by A. Martinet in the fourth chapter of his *Elements* ...

[70] Cf. *supra*, II.1.4.

[71] This may prove to be the case with all signs of connotation (cf. *infra*, Ch. IV).

[72] Broadly speaking, an exclamation (*oh*) may seem to be a syntagm made of a single unit, but in fact speech must here be restored to its context: the exclamation is an answer to a 'silent' syntagm. Cf. K. L. Pike: *Language in Relation to a*

Unified Theory of the Structure of Human Behaviour (Glendale, 1951).

[13] Saussure, quoted by R. Godel, *Les sources manuscrites du Cours de Linguistique Générale de F. de Saussure* (Droz-Minard, 1957), p. 90.

[14] A. Martinet, *Economie des changements phonétiques* (Francke, Berne, 1955), p. 22.

[15] Saussure, quoted by Godel, op. cit., p. 55.

[16] Ibid., p. 196.

[17] Cf. Frei's analysis of the sub-phonemes, *supra*, II.1.2.

[18] The phenomenon appears clearly at the level of a (monolingual) dictionary: the dictionary seems to give a positive definition of a word; but as this definition is itself made up of words which must themselves be explained, the positivity is endlessly referred further. Cf. J. Laplanche and S. Leclaire, 'L'inconscient', in *Temps Modernes*, no. 183, July 1961.

[19] *Cahiers Ferdinand de Saussure*, IX, pp. 11–40.

[80] All the oppositions suggested by Cantineau are binary.

[81] This is also a privative opposition.

[82] The economics of linguistics teaches us that there is a constant proportion beween the quantity of information to be transmitted and the energy (the time) which is necessary for this transmission (A. Martinet, *Travaux de l'Institut de Linguistique*, I, p. 11).

[83] Saussure, *Cours de linguistique générale*, p. 124.

[84] H. Frei, *Cahiers Ferdinand de Saussure*, XI, p. 35.

[85] *Destouches*, Logistique, p. 73.

[86] Cl. Lévi-Strauss, 'Introduction à l'œuvre de M. Mauss', in M. Mauss, *Sociologie et Anthropologie* (P.U.F., 1950), L, note.

[87] Cf. *Writing Degree Zero*.

[88] In *stallion/mare*, the common element is on the plane of the signified.

[89] Cantineau has not kept the *gradual oppositions*, postulated by Trubetzkoy (in German: *u/o* and *ü/ö*).

[90] Cf. R. Barthes, *Système de la Mode*, Seuil (1967).

[91] We shall not touch here on the question of the order of the terms in a paradigm; for Saussure, this order is indifferent; for Jakobson, on the contrary, in a flexion, the nominative or zero-case is the initial case (*Essais* . . ., p. 71, 'Typological studies and their contribution to historical comparative linguistics', in *Proceedings of the VIIIth International Congress of Linguists, 1957* (Oslo), pp. 17–25, Chapter III of *Essais de Linguistique Générale*). This question can become very important on the day when the metaphor, for instance, is

studied as a paradigm of signifiers, and when it has to be decided whether one term in the series has some sort of precedence. Cf. R. Barthes, 'La Métaphore de l'œil', in *Critique*, nos. 195–6, August–September 1963, and *Essais Critiques* (Seuil, 1954).

[92] *Cours de Linguistique générale*, p. 174. Course in General Linguistics, p. 126.

[93] *Preliminaries to Speech Analysis* (Cambridge, Mass.), 1952.

[94] *Économie des changements phonétiques*, 3, 15, p. 73.

[95] More rudimentary senses, like smell and taste, however, seem to be 'analogical'. Cf. V. Bélévitch, *Langage des machines et langage humain*, pp. 74–5.

[96] *Cahiers de Lexicologie*, I, 1959 ('Unité sémantique complexe et neutralisation').

[97] It is of course the *discourse* of the fashion magazine which carries out the neutralization; the latter consists, in fact, in passing from the exclusive disjunction of the AUT type (chandail *or alternatively* sweater) to the inclusive disjunction of the VEL type (chandail or sweater *indifferently*).

[98] *Cahiers Ferdinand de Saussure*, IX, pp. 41–6.

[99] Cf. J. Laplanche et S. Leclaire, art. cit.

[100] Cf. R. Barthes, 'L'activité structuraliste', in *Essais Critiques* (Seuil, 1964), p. 213.

[101] Formulated by A. Martinet, *Élements* . . ., p. 37. *Elements of General Linguistics*, p. 40.

BIBLIOGRAPHY

Semiology cannot at the present time produce an autonomous bibliography; the main books must necessarily bear upon the work of linguists, ethnologists and sociologists who refer back to structuralism or the semantic model. We present here a limited selection of works (taken from the Gonthier edition of this book) which provide a good introduction to semiological analysis.

ALLARD, M., ELZIÈRE, M., GARDIN, J. C., HOURS, F., *Analyse conceptuelle du Coran sur cartes perforées*, Paris, La Haye, Mouton & Co., 1963, Vol. I, Code, 110 pp., Vol II, Commentary, 187 pp.

BARTHES, R., *Mythologies*, Paris, ed. du Seuil, 1957, 270 pp.

BRØNDAL, V., *Essais de Linguistique générale*, Copenhagen, 1943, Munksgaard, XII, 172 pp.

BUYSSENS, E., *Les Langages et le discours, Essai de linguistique fonctionnelle dans le cadre de la sémiologie*, Brussels, 1943, Office de Publicité, 97 pp.

ERLICH, V., *Russian Formalism*, Mouton & Co., s'Gravenhage, 1955, XIV, 276 pp.

GODEL, R., *Les sources manuscrites du Cours de Linguistique générale de F. de Saussure*, Geneva, Droz, Paris, Minard, 1957, 283 pp.

GRANGER, G. G., *Pensée formelle et sciences de l'homme*, Paris, Aubier, ed. Montaigne, 1960, 226 pp.

HARRIS, Z. S., *Methods in Structural Linguistics*, University of Chicago Press, Chicago, 1951, XV, 384 pp.

HJELMSLEV, L., *Essais Linguistiques*, Travaux du Cercle Linguistique de Copenhague, vol. XIII,

Copenhagen, Nordisk Sprog- og Kulturforlag. 1959, 276 pp.

JAKOBSON, R., *Essais de Linguistique Générale*, éd. de Minuit, Paris, 1963, 262 pp.
The full title of each essay quoted is given in the notes.

LEVI-STRAUSS, C., *Anthropologie Structurale*, Paris, Plon, 1958, II, 454 pp. *Structural Anthropology*, translated by Claire Jacobson and Brooke Grundfest Schoepf, Basic Books, New York and London, 1963, 410 pp.

MARTINET, A., *Éléments de Linguistique Générale*, Paris, A. Colin, 1960, 224 pp. *Elements of General Linguistics*, translated by Elisabeth Palmer, Faber & Faber, 1964, 205 pp.

MOUNIN, G., *Les Problèmes théoriques de la traduction*, Paris, Gallimard, 1963, XII, 301 pp.

MORRIS., C. W., *Signs, Language and Behaviour*, New York, Prentice-Hall Inc., 1946, XIII, 365 pp.

PEIRCE, C. S., *Selected Writings*, ed. by J. Buchlev, Harcourt, Bruce & Co., New York, London, 1940.

PIKE, K. L., *Language in Relation to a Unified Theory of the Structure of Human Behavior*, Glendale, Calif., 3 fasc. 1954, 1955, 1960, 170–85–146 pp.

PROPP, V., 'Morphology of the Folktale,' *Intern. Journal of American Linguistics*, vol. 24; no. 4, Oct. 1958, Indiana University, X, 134 pp.

SAUSSURE, F. de, *Cours de Linguistique Générale*, Paris, Payot, 4th edition, 1949, 331 pp. *Course of General Linguistics*, transl. W. Baskin, New York Library, and Peter Owen, London, 1960.

TRUBETZKOY, N. S., *Principes de Phonologie*, translated by J. Cantineau, Klincksiek, Paris, 1957, 1st edition, 1949, XXXIV, 396 pp.

For recent developments in structural linguistics, the reader is referred to N. Ruwet's important article: 'La Linguistique générale aujourd'hui', in *Arch. europ. de Soc.*, V (1964), pp. 277–310.

SELECTED BIBLIOGRAPHY

A list of the principal works of Roland Barthes, with the date of their first appearance

LE DEGRÉ ZÉRO DE L'ÉCRITURE
(Seuil, 1953)

MICHELET PAR LUI-MÊME
(Collection: *Écrivains de Toujours*, no. 19, Seuil, 1954)

MYTHOLOGIES
(Seuil, 1957)

SUR RACINE
(Seuil, 1963)

ESSAIS CRITIQUES
(Seuil, 1964)

'ÉLÉMENTS DE SÉMIOLOGIE'
(*Communications*, no. 4, Seuil, 1964)

CRITIQUE ET VÉRITÉ
(Seuil, 1966)

A much fuller 'Bibliographie critique', covering all the aspects dealt with by all the studies contained in *Communications* No. 4, can be found in that periodical. *Communications* No. 8, which is devoted to 'The Structural Analysis of the Narrative', also contains a 'Bibliographie critique'.

INDEX

INDEX

8 7 00

NORMANDALE COMMUNITY COLLEGE
LIBRARY
9700 FRANCE AVENUE SOUTH
BLOOMINGTON MN 55431-4399